Billy

Billy

BILLY CARTER'S REFLECTIONS ON HIS STRUGGLE WITH FAME, ALCOHOLISM AND CANCER

By Billy and Sybil Carter
with Ken Estes

Edgehill Publications
NEWPORT, RHODE ISLAND

Edgehill Publications
200 Harrison Avenue
Newport, Rhode Island 02840
(401) 849-5700

ISBN:
(paper) 0-926028-05-7
(cloth) 0-926028-07-3
LC: 89-081220

To Kim, Jana, Buddy, Marle, Mandy and Earl for your love and understanding.

"WLYTG"
Mama and Daddy

FOREWORD

Welcome to Sybil's and Billy's kitchen. When you come into the house by the front door you will walk down a small hallway and turn left. If you are lucky enough to be a guest (and in this book you are), you will see a kitchen done in early American. You feel at home right away. The sun is shining through the window and you can see where Billy has planted his flowers. They are blooming.

Billy is still alive (in this book he is) and he sits across from you wearing a pair of walking shorts and a T-shirt. He has his bare foot in his hand and is making wisecracks about the breakfast Sybil is preparing. She is cooking and managing the conversation at the same time. She is also attempting to curb Billy's colorful language without success. Occasionally, the phone rings and Billy grabs it and good-naturedly raises hell with whomever happens to be calling.

Billy is not a big coffee drinker but he has a cup and if prompted takes off on world politics, local and national current events, baseball and anything else that comes to mind. Billy, as you will discover, is well read and can talk about almost anything that interests you. He tells hilarious tales about his drinking days and just as quickly comes down on drinking and sings the praises of sobriety. This is no nonsense talk. "If you think you have a problem, you have a problem," he says.

While you enjoy your food, the children, sisters, friends, in-laws, and Sybil will take turns telling you about the life they have lived. Some of it is funny and some of it is tragic, but all of it is honest and unpretentious.

When you think your coffee is getting cold Billy's brother Jimmy strolls by (he lives next door). Jimmy Carter is a quiet and gentle man with lines in his face that were not there a few years ago. And like the rest of the Carter clan he is straightforward and honest about his past. He has an occasional twinkle in his eye if he suspects that you like him. William Faulkner, for all of his genius, could not have invented the people you will meet at this breakfast table. A grand and glorious Southern family in triumph and tragedy. But that's too much of that kind of talk. As an American living at home, you need this book. As a visitor to these grand shores, you will understand us better.

Thanks for the coffee, Sybil, and to Ken Estes who helped out in the kitchen.

Tom T. Hall
Franklin, Tennessee
May 1989

CHAPTER ONE

August 1988

I woke up in my hospital bed at the National Cancer Institute late at night on June 4 to find two doctors hovering over my bed.

I didn't realize it at the time, but I had been in a coma for three days. A few minutes earlier, the doctors had been discussing whether I would ever come out of it.

Once they discovered I was awake, one of my doctors (Dr. Steven Rosenberg) began asking me over and over again if I knew my name.

I said, "Damn right, I do. My name is Billy Carter."

Then he asked me if I knew where I was. I told him, "No," but I needed to use the phone to call my wife Sybil.

While I had been in the coma, I had dreamed that Sybil had bought a brand new red convertible and had wrecked it before I had a chance to drive it.

The trouble was I didn't know it was a dream. I wanted to call Sybil and give her a piece of my mind for buying the car in the first place.

When I got in touch with Sybil a few minutes later at the hotel where she was staying nearby, she started crying.

She had been at my bedside for the last three days and had thought the end was near.

I decided to wait until the next day to ask her about the car.

* * *

I learned later that during my treatment at the National Cancer Institute in Bethesda, Maryland, doctors had given up hope for me three times. I'm getting used to that. Twice before in a period of nine months, my doctors told me there was nothing else they could do for me.

I have pancreatic cancer, and I know all too well my chances of surviving for any length of time are slim and none. But I've beaten the odds so far. It's August of 1988 now, and I've lasted more than 11 months since the time bomb inside me started ticking.

The first time I fooled the doctors was when my cancer was

diagnosed at Emory University in Atlanta in September of 1987. They discovered the cancer was inoperable, and thought I wouldn't live more than three or four months. But we learned about a radical form of treatment using radiation and chemotherapy, and that treatment carried me into early spring.

In April, tests showed that the treatment had slowed the growth of the tumor but hadn't killed the cancer cells. My doctor (Dr. Martin York) was sympathetic, but said there was very little more he could do. He had already done a lot by keeping me alive that long, but I was not ready to quit yet.

Over Dr. York's objections, I found a doctor in South Carolina willing to treat me with interferon. But only hours before I was to begin that treatment, my brother Jimmy intervened. He had talked to Dr. Armand Hammer (chairman of Occidental Petroleum Company and a great benefactor of the National Cancer Institute) and had arranged for me to meet with Dr. Rosenberg to determine if I might be a candidate for an experimental cancer treatment program Dr. Rosenberg was using at the Institute. The drug used in the treatment is called Interleukin-2.

After a lot of tests, Dr. Rosenberg accepted me as one of the first pancreatic cancer patients to undergo the treatment. I remember him patiently explaining to me all the risks involved in the treatment—heart failure, fluid build-up and the like — but he needn't have bothered.

I felt like I had a new lease on life, even though the odds were still 9 or 10 to 1 against a cure. The way I looked at it, those odds were a lot better than I would have had without treatment.

* * *

As it turned out, the side-effects of the Interleukin-2 treatment were as bad as Dr. Rosenberg had said.

I was not able to complete a full course of treatment because I became ill with high fever and a virus and lapsed into the coma.

But the treatment I did have resulted in a slight reduction in the size of the tumor, and if I can gain some strength back, I am scheduled to return to Bethesda for another session in October.

That is, if the cancer doesn't get me first. Realistically, I've got a long way to go before I get my strength back. On top of everything else, I've developed an ulcer, and my weight has dropped all the way down to 125 pounds from about 180.

CHAPTER ONE

I'm in a race against time, and I have no illusions about it.

The biggest fear I've had in my fight with cancer is the thought of being kept alive by heroic means.

I made Sybil and my doctors promise not to plug me into respirators and machines just to keep me breathing.

I would try the most radical treatment imaginable. Even a voodoo doctor. But under no circumstances do I want to be kept alive by artificial means.

Something like that would be too hard on my family.

* * *

Some people, including my brother Jimmy, have praised my courage and grace in my battle with cancer. That's the first time I've ever been accused of having grace. I really think what's kept me going is my stubbornness.

As we say in the South, I'm bad stubborn. Ask anyone who knows me.

If you want me to do something, just tell me I can't do it. My stubbornness helped me quit drinking in 1979. No one, not even the staff at the alcoholism treatment hospital where I stayed for eight weeks, thought I could quit drinking. The only person who had any faith in me was Mike Brubaker, one of my counselors in treatment. He's just as stubborn as I am, and I guess he knew how to appreciate that quality in me.

I quit drinking for three years just to prove everybody wrong, and finally, began to realize that sobriety was a pretty good way to go. Actually, my friends in Alcoholics Anonymous had been telling me that for three years, but, as I said, I'm bad stubborn, which isn't always a virtue. Besides, I'm a slow learner. It took me eight weeks to complete a three-week treatment program for alcoholism at the Long Beach Naval Hospital.

I haven't had a drink for more than nine years now. That's probably the thing in my life of which I'm proudest.

If I hadn't stopped drinking, I would have been dead long ago. I was drinking a half gallon of vodka a day right before I quit. So in a way, I've been living on borrowed time. My sister Gloria says I look better now—cancer and all—than I did when I was drinking. I guess I have to agree with her.

Unfortunately, I have less control over my cancer than I do my drinking. I'll live only as long as medical science will permit. But the principles I've learned in staying sober have helped me deal with cancer.

I'm living one day at a time and putting my trust in God, or my Higher Power as we call Him in A.A.

This spring I was talking to a black minister in Plains about miracles, and I asked him if God still performed miracles. You may remember that my sister Ruth (who died of pancreatic cancer in 1983) was a faith healer, who believed very strongly in miracles.

The minister thought a while and said:

"He sure does, Mr. Billy. The only thing different is He uses His doctors and His medicine to perform them."

That sounded like a pretty good philosophy to me.

* * *

Some people I've met on my travels since I became sick look at me like they've just seen a ghost. A couple of them have admitted to me that they thought I had died.

I tell them I hope I haven't disappointed them.

This spring a little boy in Plains told me that he thought I sure looked good. But, he added that he thought another man in Plains had sure looked good, too, right before he died.

His mother, who was with him, was embarrassed, but I broke up laughing. I thought it was funny.

I haven't minded at all talking about my cancer or about dying. Sybil and the kids get on me at times for being ghoulish. Sometimes maybe I have gone too far, but it's my way of dealing with the situation. I don't want people to treat me with kid gloves.

Reporters have a reputation for being insensitive, but those who have interviewed me since I became sick seem more hesitant about talking about my cancer than I am.

Before I was interviewed by a talk show host in Florida last winter, she asked me if I had any reservations about answering questions concerning "my illness." I replied, "If you mean my cancer, no. Fire away."

Since I developed cancer, I've been blindsided by the media only once as Sybil and I have gone around the country talking about alcoholism at alcohol and drug treatment centers.

A columnist in Chicago criticized me for my smoking habit. He said it contradicted my message about my recovery from alcoholism and my fight with cancer. If he had given me a chance to respond, I would have told him nobody's perfect.

As a matter of fact, I started smoking again for only a few weeks between the end of my treatment at Emory University Hospital and the beginning of treatment at the National Cancer Institute. Once Dr. Rosenberg gave me the signal before starting treatment at Bethesda, I quit cold turkey.

Otherwise, the media have been good to me. They've given me the chance to spread the message about recovery from alcoholism and how my recovery has helped me deal with cancer.

I've had sort of a love-hate relationship with the media since the day Jimmy was elected president in 1976.

They've got a job to do, and it's tough. But they get carried away with their own importance at times.

For example, I always thought Sam Donaldson (who has become famous for his badgering of presidents as a newsman for ABC) was one of the nicest people you'd ever meet when you were off-camera, one-on-one. But the minute the camera started rolling, Sam could get tough as nails.

* * *

I can't stress enough how my recovery from alcoholism has helped me deal with cancer. The one day at a time, turn it over to God philosophy of A.A. can help you face most any problem in life.

Sybil has probably followed this philosophy even more religiously than I have and has passed it on to our six kids and their families. She says time and time again that the Twelve Step program has been her salvation since my cancer was diagnosed.

Sybil took part in a program at Long Beach Naval Hospital for families of alcoholics at the same time I was in treatment.

Basically, she learned how not to take any crap from me. And, believe you me, her treatment took. I tell people that Sybil was a nice Southern lady when she went into treatment, and a double-barreled bitch when she came out. I smile when I say it.

Sybil and I have been close to the subject of alcoholism for the past several years. We speak a lot and have met a lot of other speakers and experts in the alcohol field.

My message is pretty simple: If I can get sober, anybody can.

People sure as hell remember my drinking. I was the most public drunk in America when Jimmy was president.

Lee Karns, president of the CareUnit treatment system, kids me about my owing a debt to society for giving Billy Beer to the world. He calls Billy Beer the Edsel of beers.

Seriously, I think people can relate to me and my story. Who's some good ol' boy redneck going to relate to when he winds up in jail dead drunk and can't remember what he did to get there? Elizabeth Taylor? Betty Ford? A psychiatrist? Or me?

With all the information in the world on alcohol and drugs (television commercials, books, movies, billboards and the like), it always surprises me that people still don't know what to do or where to turn when they need help for themselves or someone else.

We've got an unlisted telephone number, but a couple of people a week, from all over the country, manage to locate Sybil or me to get our advice on an alcohol problem. I've even been approached by people in airports and hotel lobbies.

I always tell them the same thing: "If you think there's a problem, there is a problem. Go get some help."

* * *

A couple of other questions have kept cropping up since I developed cancer.

One question is: "Since you've got inoperable cancer, what difference does it make whether you drink or not?"

Well, the answer is really pretty simple. The thought of drinking again never occurred to me.

I want to enjoy whatever's left of my life and to be close with my family and friends. If I drank, I couldn't enjoy those things. I'm an alcoholic, and I can never return to what people refer to as normal drinking. When I drink, I get drunk. There's no in-between for me, or for any alcoholic.

While I was drinking, I was a miserable husband, father, son and brother. Why would I want to return to that—cancer or no cancer?

A friend of mine who was trying hard to stay sober told me a story about a man he met at an A.A. meeting who was dying from cancer. The man told him that he was grateful for at least one thing: he was going to die sober, around friends and family who cared. The man said if he'd died drunk seven years earlier, no one would have cared. In fact, they probably would have been relieved.

My friend said that man's story has helped him stay sober for more than five years now.

That's how A.A. works. One drunk helping another.

* * *

The other question is: "Did your drinking cause your cancer?"

Doctors tell me, no. But I really don't know.

The doctors also say that there is no evidence that pancreatic cancer is hereditary. All I know is that my father and my sister died of pancreatic cancer, so I'm not quite ready to rule out heredity.

Whatever, I want researchers to find out all they can about pancreatic cancer—for the sake of my kids, and the rest of our family.

I'm hopeful that my case and the treatment I've gone through will help cancer research in some way.

CHAPTER TWO

In no way do I want to imply I've been a model of courage this past year. I'm not ready for sainthood.

There have been times that I have been real depressed, and times when I just didn't give a damn whether I lived or died. But there's always been just enough fight left in me to keep going.

I figure if I keep putting up a brave front, pretty soon I'll start to believe it myself.

I've been scared at times. I've woken up in the middle of the night in a cold sweat, frightened out of my wits. I'm sure I was having nightmares about dying, but fortunately I don't remember them. I would feel a tightness in my chest and have difficulty breathing. It was always a relief to realize I was awake and alive, but I sure didn't want to go back to sleep.

In November and December of 1987, as much as I wanted to go home, I dreaded leaving the hospital. I didn't think I could survive away from the hospital. I had gone home twice from Emory University Hospital, but both times, I had become so sick that I thought I was going to die then and there. The only place I felt safe was in the hospital.

In November, on one of my visits home, my youngest son, Earl, who was 11 at the time, and I took a walk together near the pond between Jimmy's house and ours. I believed it was the last time we would have a chance to be together by ourselves.

I'm grateful I was wrong. During the nine months since then, Earl and I have had a lot of good times together. We've developed a ritual of feeding the fish in the pond in the afternoon and playing baseball in the front yard whenever I was able.

Earl and I went to the Atlanta Braves season-opener with the Cubs. The Braves blew a big lead and lost in extra innings, but Earl enjoyed the game anyway.

The Braves went on to lose their first 10 games and are a lead-pipe-cinch to finish in last place.

I told a friend the other day that I had had a bad year in 1988, but not as bad as the Braves.

* * *

From the time my cancer was diagnosed in September, my main concern has been for Earl. Growing up without a father is tough. I know. Daddy died of pancreatic cancer when I was 16, and it turned my life upside down. After Daddy died, I was as close to being a juvenile delinquent as we had in Plains. It's a wonder I didn't wind up in prison.

I'm sure Earl won't react to my death that way.

In this past year, I've tried to be a real father to Earl in every way I could without babying him.

In July, when Sybil and I were speaking at the opening of a new hospital in Tampa, Florida, we took Earl with us, and we spent several days on the beach at St. Petersburg not far from where Sybil and I stayed on our honeymoon 33 years earlier.

Earl was the first of our children to hear our speech about our problems with alcoholism. The people at the hospital taped our talk so all of our kids could hear it.

My talk, in particular, doesn't pull many punches.

Afterward I asked Earl if he had been embarrassed listening to me in front of so many people. He said, no, by now he was used to the way I talked.

Anyway, I think he was feeling a little smug because he had beaten me in miniature golf the day before.

I want Earl to finish college, which I never did, and to be happy. He's a lot better kid than I was at his age. The same's true for all six of our children.

I'm not concerned about any of them. The next youngest, Mandy, who's 20, is on her way to completing college at Georgia Southwestern in Americus. Kim (the eldest) and Marle are both schoolteachers and are expecting babies. And our son Buddy, who lives in Nashville, is doing well. He is planning to start a landscaping business.

Our second oldest child, Jana, who everyone says is more like me than the others, is finally finding her way, and I don't worry about her anymore. Jana had a malignant growth removed from her leg at Emory University Hospital in January of 1987, but there has been no recurrence. Jana and I have been to Emory together for check-ups, and I think she's a lot more trouble to deal with as a patient than I am. It doesn't take much to make her mad. Wonder where she got that from?

CHAPTER TWO

Since I've gotten sober, my temper has gotten out of control only once. I was furious at Jana's ex-husband for not treating her right, and once if I could have gotten my hands on a gun, I might have shot him. One thing I won't put up with is someone messing with my kids.

Really, I'm not very dangerous with a gun. One night, a bunch of us were raising hell and shooting at the water tower in Plains. I never hit it once.

* * *

Mandy is our only other child living at home, although Jana and Kim both live close by in Plains. Mandy and I have become a lot closer, too, in the last few months. Mandy and Earl don't remember much about my drinking, and the older kids think Mandy and Earl have had it a lot easier than they did. They're right, of course, but I'll never admit it to them.

Sybil has been a good mother to the kids, and that's one reason I don't worry about how they'll do when I'm gone.

I took Mandy on a trip with me to Los Angeles in May for an appearance on a television talk show. The host encouraged her to come on the show with me, and she did, although I think she was embarrassed.

I let Mandy go out to a nightclub with a young man she met in Los Angeles, and our older girls couldn't believe it. I wouldn't even let them wear make-up when they were teenagers.

I also took Mandy with me to the Democratic Convention in Atlanta on July 19. I had a choice of either going on July 18, when Jimmy was scheduled to speak, or on July 19, when Jesse Jackson was scheduled. I never told Jimmy I had a choice. I wanted to hear Jesse. I thought his speech would be history-in-the-making.

I had supported Jesse, even though I doubted seriously he could win. But I knew Jesse would shake everyone up and be a champion for the little people. Jesse had called me in the hospital in Atlanta in October 1987 to ask me if he could count on my support. I didn't hesitate. I told Jesse that every black needed a Southern redneck in his campaign.

Because of my health, I was able to make only one appearance for Jesse (at a Teamsters Union meeting in Atlanta), but I made sure I voiced my support for him in every interview I did. I told

Tom Snyder on his radio show in Los Angeles that Jesse was going to surprise a lot of people in the Super Tuesday primary in March, and damned if I wasn't right.

Jimmy never formally endorsed any candidate for the nomination, but I know he was thrilled that Jesse did so well. You may have noticed Jesse recognized Jimmy in his speech, and Michael Dukakis didn't. I sure noticed.

I wasn't excited by any of the other Democratic candidates. I have suspected all along that George Bush would win in November.

A lot of people who hadn't seen me for a few months said they were shocked at how I looked on television during the convention. I'm not surprised. My ulcer was acting up, my suit was a few sizes too big, and I felt real tired.

But I'm glad I heard Jesse's speech. That's what politics should be like.

* * *

Sybil and I made a decision early on in my illness that I should continue to keep an active schedule as long as I could. And, thanks to my employer, Ocilla Industries, and some speaking engagements, I've been able to do just that.

How's this for timing? Just a few days before my cancer was diagnosed, I had agreed to make a number of appearances at CareUnit treatment centers across the country and had decided to quit my job with the modular home division of Ocilla Industries in Ocilla, Georgia. I wanted to devote full time to speaking and some other business. Fortunately, my medical insurance was still in effect when I learned I had cancer. Since my hospital bills were astronomical, you can imagine what that meant.

Later, I was able to go into work occasionally, and I appeared for Ocilla at two modular home trade shows in the spring. Even at that, my boss, Roger Snow, president of Ocilla, insisted that if I didn't feel up to it, I shouldn't try to appear at the trade shows.

CompCare, which operates the CareUnit alcohol and drug treatment system, was accommodating, too. They let Sybil pinch-hit for me in St. Louis and Cincinnati while I was in the hospital and booked me for speeches around my treatment schedule. The people in St. Louis and Cincinnati don't know how lucky they were. Sybil's a better speaker than I am.

CHAPTER TWO

My first public appearance after leaving Emory was at CareUnit of Orlando in December. It was my second appearance in Orlando, and they dedicated a room at the hospital in honor of Sybil and me.

At all of my speeches—good or bad—Sybil and I got a standing ovation. I can't begin to tell you how that made me feel.

I thought that maybe all the thousands of people who saw us in person or on television, or read about us in the paper, didn't regard me as the president's idiot brother anymore. And that maybe I helped someone with a problem.

I sure hope so.

* * *

I talked to a lot of people in need of help on those trips to the hospitals.

At CareUnit of Los Angeles, my old alcoholism counselor Mike Brubaker pulled me aside and asked me to talk to a young kid who was thinking about leaving treatment after only a few days.

I told the kid that I had hated treatment when I first got there and that it had taken me three or four weeks in the hospital before I decided I wanted to stay. I even had an airline ticket to London in my pocket for the first few days. I asked the kid to just stick it out a little longer to see what happened.

Mike told me later that the boy finished treatment and was doing fine when he had last talked to him.

At CareUnit of South Florida in Tampa in July, a woman, whose father had pancreatic cancer and whose husband was recovering from alcoholism, came to see Sybil and me at the hospital before our speech later that afternoon. We talked for about a half hour, and I think it helped all of us.

And in the question-and-answer part of our speech in Tampa, a man in the audience who had just discovered he had pancreatic cancer asked me for any advice I could give him. There were 500 people in the room, but you could hear a pin drop when the man spoke. I don't know if my response helped him, but I thought he showed a lot of courage by asking the question in a room full of strangers.

* * *

I'll talk to about anybody who wants to talk to me about alcoholism and cancer. It's good therapy for me.

I try to approach everything with a sense of humor and as honestly as I can. There's no use trying to soft-soap the truth to a recovering alcoholic or a cancer victim. We don't have time for it.

I liked the way my doctors arranged chemotherapy sessions. They are like mini A.A. meetings. I never received my treatment by myself. There was always another patient there, and we'd always start talking. It helped us all. Otherwise, we'd have been sitting there feeling sorry for ourselves.

I also built a relationship over the telephone with a pancreatic cancer patient in Tennessee. Our friends, Tom T. and Dixie Hall in Nashville, set it up. The man in Tennessee and I talked together a lot, sometimes up to a half hour or so at a time.

There also have been a lot of funny moments.

I was walking down the hallway at Emory University Hospital once, when this old man stopped me and asked if I was Billy Carter. I thought he was going to sympathize with me for having cancer, but he said, "Bet your cancer ain't near as bad as my brother's."

Speaking of getting no sympathy, the morning I was going into surgery at Emory to find out what the growth in my abdomen was, my friend Don Carter (who is no relation) stopped by to see me and chased everybody else out so we could play liar's poker. And the S.O.B. cheated. But I beat him out of $60. He probably thought he wouldn't have to pay up if I died in surgery. And he's my best friend.

CHAPTER THREE

All I thought I had was the itch when I went to the doctor in Americus last September.

I itched like crazy. I had been taking a couple of showers a day to get some relief, but I thought it would just go away in time. I had had a similar problem a few years earlier that was caused by some type of allergy.

I didn't feel bad at all. As a matter of fact, I was feeling pretty good. I had just lost about 20 pounds, and I was making plans for the future. I had just gotten back from Los Angeles, where I had gone to tape an ice cream commercial playing off my reputation as beer-drinking good ol' boy. I also was talking to a publisher about a book, and I had made arrangements for a number of speaking engagements. Everything looked pretty good for me.

Sybil had insisted I go to the doctor. She had come back from a trip to Nashville and had started telling me that I didn't look good. She said my skin looked yellow. Frances Irlbeck (my former secretary) said the same thing when she saw me at supper in Plains one night. I told Frances and Sybil they were didn't know what they were talking about. But finally I had agreed to go the doctor because the itch was driving me nuts.

Later, Kim, Jana—everybody—told me how worried they had been about the way I looked. And here I was thinking I looked great.

That's the way us alcoholics think, drunk or sober. We look at ourselves and the world a little bit different than other people do.

* * *

My doctor, Harvey Simpson, brought me to reality in a hurry. He thought I might have either hepatitis or some other liver problem and admitted me to Sumter County Hospital in Americus for tests. He said he hoped I had hepatitis instead of something worse. He didn't have to tell me what that something worse was.

The tests in Americus showed a mass in the abdomen, and I was transferred to Emory University Hospital for more tests and surgery.

I tried not to think about the worst, but it was nearly impossible.

Thirty-four years earlier, we had taken Daddy to Emory University Hospital for exploratory surgery. They had found pancreatic cancer and had just sewed him back up and sent him home to die. He had died three months later. And my sister Ruth hadn't done any better in 1983 when they discovered she had cancer.

I consoled myself by remembering Daddy and Ruth had both been in bad pain when they went to the hospital. I hadn't felt a lick of pain. Not yet anyway.

* * *

The next few days were like a nightmare.

Sure enough, they found I had pancreatic cancer. And sure enough, it was inoperable, just like it had been with Daddy and Ruth.

I had trouble accepting all this at first. I was mad as hell, then sad as hell. I never thought I would be the type of person to ask: "Why me?" But, I did. Finally, though, I started to come around—mentally, at least. I accepted the fact I had cancer, but I didn't accept the fact I was going to die. I made up my mind to fight it.

Through all this, things were probably harder on Sybil and the children than they were on me.

I was out of it a lot of the time with pain-killers and sedatives. The doctors couldn't operate on the tumor, which was about the size of a fist. But that didn't stop them from rearranging my stomach. It took two operations to finish the job, which was some sort of pancreatic bypass procedure.

My recovery from the surgery was tough, which was funny in a way. The surgery was done to improve the quality of my life and maybe prolong it a little. It almost killed me.

But at least it took my mind off the cancer.

* * *

I had planned to be back home in October, but I was in the hospital from September to early December—first, for recuperation from the surgery and finally, for a couple of two-week sessions of radiation therapy and chemotherapy.

Nothing seemed to be going right, and like I said earlier, about November I began to doubt whether I would ever leave the hospital alive. I found out later that few people, if any, thought I would ever get to come home. I never asked Sybil if she thought I would go home, and she never told me.

I would get a virus. A tube would pop out. Or I would get sick at my stomach. I was nauseated almost the whole time I was at Emory. I couldn't eat solid food for about 10 weeks. I was fed through a tube implanted in my intestines.

At one point, I had so many tubes in me I looked like a porcupine.

Still, the worst thing for me was the effect of the pain-killers. I felt like I was drunk. I was seeing bugs on the wall and talking to people who weren't there. That really bothered me, and I told them to hold back on my medication if possible. I didn't want to become a junkie.

The whole thing reminded me of when I was detoxing from booze in 1979. It had taken me 11 days to detox. That scared the hell out of me, but at the end of the 11 days, I still wasn't convinced that I was an alcoholic.

* * *

Sybil was at my side in the hospital from the time I went in until I finished my chemotherapy after the first of the year. She had a rollaway bed moved into the room and acted as my watchdog, interpreter and public relations person. It was a role she took to naturally. She had done the same thing when I was drinking and raising hell. The only difference was she didn't take any lip from me this time.

Sybil would tell me to shut up and do what I was told. I couldn't argue too much because I was afraid she would put an air bubble in one of my tubes.

Some of the children and grandchildren were there every weekend. Marle and Jody must have driven down from Charlotte a dozen times, and Buddy, Marlene and Little Will (their three-year-old son) came down from Nashville almost as much. The others drove up from Plains, which is about three hours south of Atlanta by car.

I had told the kids it wasn't necessary to visit so much. But I'm glad they did. I wanted to be as close to them as I could. The only real regret I have about my drinking days is the hurt it caused my family. I don't think I can ever make up for that.

Jimmy came by about every day he was in Atlanta, where he has an office at the Presidential Center. He would usually drop off a stack of books for me to read. I like to read (I used to read two or three books a day), but some of the books Jimmy brought were pretty heavy stuff. I had to force myself to read the books because I knew Jimmy would want to talk about them the next time he came by.

* * *

I don't kid myself anymore about Jimmy's influence on my life. I probably wouldn't be alive today if he hadn't been president.

I wouldn't have had access to the cancer treatment I've had without his connections. That's not a put down of my doctors at Emory, which is one of the best hospitals in the country. They favored a conservative approach to treatment, which would have made it much easier on me physically than the approach I chose. The only trouble was I probably would have died within a few months. We'll never know, of course.

But I didn't want to die easy; I wanted to go for it—even if it was a million to one shot.

Still, Dr. York at Emory was willing to try a more radical type of chemotherapy and radiation treatment using platinum. It had never been used at Emory before. Jimmy had learned of the treatment by talking to experts at the National Cancer Institute and Mount Sinai Hospital in New York.

The treatment was three two-week doses of radiation and chemotherapy, with two weeks off between treatments.

The platinum used in the treatment was pretty expensive. I told Sybil to see if she could recover the platinum if I died.

* * *

I thought for sure I would lose my hair during the treatment. But for some reason I didn't.

While I was in the hospital, I joked about shaving my head just to prove to an old lady in Plains that I really had cancer. I could just hear her saying, "See, I told you that no good Billy Carter had AIDS."

I like living in Plains, but some people there probably would just as soon I lived somewhere else. Some people in Plains flat out don't like me. They don't like Jimmy either. But no one would ever tell us to our face.

It's typical small-town stuff. In Jimmy's case, it's probably jealousy. With me, it's different; the dislike goes back to my days of guzzling beer in front of the service station, always saying what was on my mind, and generally, not giving a damn what anybody thought.

My mother (Miss Lillian) was like that—minus the drinking. It always amazed me that she could live in a small town like Plains and not give a damn what anybody thought of her. I don't know where she got that from.

Jimmy's not that way at all. He wants to be liked. I guess that's why he's a politician, and I'm not.

To my knowledge, one of the few people Jimmy couldn't bring himself to like was (Senator) Teddy Kennedy. It must have been hard for Jimmy to have a meeting with Kennedy at the Democratic Convention this year. I don't think he'll ever forget Kennedy turning his back to him on the platform at the 1980 convention.

I thought it was funny when Jimmy was quoted as saying he was "going to whip Kennedy's ass" in the 1980 primaries. A lot of people probably thought I had started coaching Jimmy.

* * *

While I was in the hospital in Atlanta, Sybil and I decided to go ahead with this book. I didn't know how much I would be able to contribute to it, but we thought it was worth a try.

I had been approached a couple of times about doing books while Jimmy was president, but I turned them down. They wanted a bunch of sensational stuff, like everybody's doing about Reagan. I didn't want to play that game.

There's honor among us good ol' boys from the South.

A couple of guys put together a paperback book about my so-called redneck humor without my help or my permission, and my sister Ruth wrote a biography about me called *Brother Billy*. If anything, Ruth's book about me was way too nice. It played down my drinking and was written before all the stuff with Libya.

I had decided to do a book about my recovery from alcoholism about a month before my cancer was diagnosed. I had flunked English 101 in college, so I hooked up with Ken Estes, a writer friend in California who barely passed 101 himself.

When Jimmy asked me how I had selected a writer, I told him: (1) it had to be someone I knew and liked; (2) it had to be someone who could understand the way I talked; (3) it had to be someone recovering from alcoholism; and (4) it had to be someone who could write.

Jimmy looked at me in amazement and said, "Billy, there probably are only one or two people in the whole world who meet your criteria."

Anyway we decided to go ahead with the book. Now, it would be about my alcoholism, my cancer, and Sybil's and my life together.

When Ken first saw me at Emory, he told me that he doubted we'd ever get the book done. He said when he walked into my room, I looked half dead. I was lying there asleep with my mouth open and about a hundred tubes sticking out of me.

I told him not to worry: a book about me would probably sell a hell of a lot better if I were dead.

* * *

When all's said and done, this is basically a story about my alcoholism, and my recovery from it. And Sybil and the kids' recovery. Drinking colored the first 24 years of Sybil's and my marriage, and most of my actions when Jimmy was in the White House.

I don't remember half the stuff I said or did when I was drinking, but Sybil and my family and friends sure do. Sybil will tell that part of the story, some of which isn't too pretty.

* * *

As I said earlier, my recovery from alcoholism has helped me deal with cancer. The opposite's also true.

During the past year, I've gotten more in touch with my sobriety and what it means to me.

On February 22, I went to a small A.A. meeting in an old converted schoolhouse in Americus, not far from the hospital where I started sobering up nine years earlier. I received a little old plastic chip—sort of like a poker chip—for what we call my ninth A.A. birthday.

For the first few years I was sober, I hadn't gone to a meeting to take a birthday chip. But that one in Americus meant a lot to me. I was alive, and I was sober.

I got another chip a few days later in Los Alamitos, California, near the Long Beach Naval Hospital where I was treated for alcoholism. Sybil and I were in Los Angeles at the time to speak at a hospital in Los Angeles.

My old counselor Mike Brubaker took me to the meeting, which was one Mike used to drag me to while I was in treatment. I saw a lot of familiar faces from nine years earlier, which must mean the meetings work.

I remember that I never would admit I was an alcoholic at those meetings nine years ago. I would always say, "My name's Billy Carter, and I drink too much." That used to drive Brubaker up the wall.

This time, though, I said, "My name's Billy Carter, and I am an alcoholic." I grinned at Brubaker when I said it.

* * *

Mike and I have become real good friends through the years, probably because he's just as insufferable as I am. He was about the only person who thought I could stay sober, but I don't think he was too sure about it himself.

He says I was the worst patient he ever had. His only problem with me today is that I tell the media I'm in A.A. He says that I'm supposed to remain anonymous in the press with regard to A.A.

I just tell him he's full of it. I was the most public drunk in the U.S., and I'm sure not going to go anonymous now.

* * *

I also had a great party for my real birthday on March 29 at Tom T. and Dixie Hall's place in Nashville.

I was feeling real good then. Probably too good.

I had actually started to think that the cancer might be in remission. While I was in treatment at Emory, I had no illusions about a cure. I was just hoping to stretch things out as long as I could. In fact, I was worried that Sybil might be setting herself for a fall by hoping for a cure.

About a week after my birthday, I was the one who got knocked for a loop when Dr. York told us in Atlanta that the treatment hadn't resulted in a remission. He said that the tumor hadn't grown, but it was just a matter of time before it started to.

I haven't permitted myself to become optimistic again. Anyway, Tom T. and Dixie surprised me with a birthday party. Sybil and I had driven up from Plains for an appearance at a modular home show for Ocilla Industries. And I was grubby-looking as hell — jeans, an old shirt and tennis shoes. Ned McWherter (the governor of Tennessee) was there along with some other politicians and the Grand Ole Opry crowd.

I should have been embarrassed by the way I looked, but Dixie pointed out that I probably wouldn't have looked any better if I had known about the party ahead of time.

Dixie and I have a lot of fun together. We're always trading insults, which sometimes shocks people around us. Our standard greeting or parting comment is "Kiss my ass."

When they were wheeling me down the hall to surgery for the first time at Emory last September, I yelled back to Dixie, "Kiss my ass." She yelled back, "Kiss my ass." The only other people who knew what was going on were Tom T. and Sybil. The rest of the people in the hallway thought we were crazy.

I also told Dixie before I went into surgery that if I died, I was going to come back to haunt her.

* * *

Back in the fall while I was at Emory, I started planning my funeral. Sybil protested, but I went on with my plans anyway. I told her if I lived, we could call the whole thing off.

I talked Tom T. into delivering my eulogy. He didn't want to talk about the funeral either, and I think he agreed just to get me to shut up. I knew he'd be perfect. I don't want a somber funeral with people standing up and telling lies about me.

If anybody's going to lie about me, I want it to be Brother Dan (Ariail), the preacher at our church (Maranatha Baptist Church). People expect preachers to lie a little bit at funerals. I remember going with my secretary Frances to the funeral of an old man who everybody hated. When the preacher started saying what a good man he was, I looked over at Frances and said:

"Let's go. I think we're at the wrong damned funeral."

* * *

When I learned I had cancer, I switched my membership from the Plains Baptist Church to Maranatha Baptist. I hadn't been too concerned about that sort of thing before, but I told Brother Dan I had better hedge all my bets.

Jimmy, Sybil and my daughter Kim are members of Maranatha, which was started up when Jimmy was president because the Plains Baptist Church refused to admit blacks. There was a big fuss about it then.

I voted with Jimmy and a few others to admit blacks to the Plains

Baptist Church, but when we lost, I didn't bother to change my membership. Heck, I never went anyway.

Funny thing about all that was that the local blacks didn't want to go to the Plains Baptist Church in the first place. They have their own church. So here's Plains, a little town of about 700 with three Baptist churches.

I've never been too religious. In fact, I didn't know Jimmy was so religious until I read it in the papers. I didn't even know he was a "born-again" Christian.

I've become a lot more spiritual in the last few years through A.A., but a little formal religion sure doesn't hurt.

What did hurt was that Jimmy and Brother Dan conned me into helping out around the church. Once after I had helped Jimmy mow the grass at the church on a hot day, I told Brother Dan that if I had known I was going to live so long, I would have waited to transfer my membership.

* * *

Despite not feeling worth much most of the time, this last year has been pretty good for me.

I have grown closer to Sybil and the kids and to Jimmy and my sister Gloria. After I got sick, Gloria and I patched up our feud, which dated back to the days when Jimmy was president.

Mandy told me that she almost fell over dead when she saw Gloria and me speaking to each other on the street in downtown Plains. I had never bothered telling anyone that Gloria and I were speaking again. As it was, we just started up again. Neither one of us ever mentioned the eight years we hadn't spoken to each other. That's the way we Carters are.

Jimmy and I have never sat down and talked about my deal with Libya. It's probably just as well. If we ever started talking about Libya, he might want to kill me.

Sybil and I probably have talked to each other more these last few months than we did in our first 32 years of marriage. I always say that she does most of the talking, but that's not really true. It's been a good year for us despite all the health problems.

* * *

Billy never returned to Bethesda, Maryland for a second Interleukin-2 treatment.

His cancer began spreading in late summer, and on the night of September 24, Billy entered a sleep from which he never awakened. He died at home at 7:06 a.m., September 25, in the company of his immediate family.

He was buried the following afternoon in the Carter family plot at the foot of his father's grave in the small Plains cemetery on the outskirts of town, not far from the spot where he was born 51 years earlier.

Tom T. Hall delivered the eulogy. The Rev. Dan Ariail and the Rev. Will Campbell also spoke.

At the request of Buddy Carter, all the men at the service were asked by Tom T. Hall to remove their ties. He said, "Billy's not wearing a tie today, and he wouldn't want you to, either."

The service concluded with a recitation of the Alcoholics Anonymous Serenity Prayer by the 500 or so mourners gathered in the small cemetery.

The words of the prayer are:

"God grant me the serenity to accept the things I cannot change; the courage to change the things I can; and the wisdom to know the difference."

* * *

Following is the story of Billy's life, as told by Billy and Sybil, with observations from the couple's six children, former President Jimmy Carter, Billy's sister, Gloria Spann, and many of Billy's closest friends.

CHAPTER FOUR

Sybil Carter

I thought, "This isn't fair!"

Here, Billy's finally gotten his life in order. He's doing something worthwhile by helping other people with alcoholism.

He's established a pretty good relationship with all the kids.

He and I have a good relationship. We're finally halfway on the same wavelength.

We're enjoying being back in Plains.

Now, he's got terminal cancer!

* * *

Those are the first thoughts that hit me when I found out Billy had inoperable cancer.

It was more like a rage.

I had feared the worst on the morning of September 11, 1987, when Billy had been taken off to surgery. But still the news struck me like a bolt of lightning. I really hadn't been prepared at all.

I never thought Billy would leave the hospital. All I knew was that I was going to be there to give him all the support he needed. I never once thought that Billy would regain his strength and that the next few months would be one of the best periods for us as a couple in our 32 years of marriage.

* * *

In this past year, Billy and I were a lot closer than ever before. It was sad that we had to reach this point to be as close as we were. But what's important is that we were closer. I'm thankful we had that chance.

When Jimmy was president, I once told a reporter that I could live with anything except maybe the death of my husband or one of my children.

But I know I can live with Billy's death. Billy told me time and time again that he knew I could live with it. I think he wanted to prepare me for the future.

I told Billy that I knew the time was going to come when he would no longer be here, and I wasn't going to like it. But I was going to carry on as best I could.

I owed that much to the children and grandchildren. Mostly, though, I owed it to myself.

* * *

I felt like I was holding my breath for the last year of Billy's life.

I prayed that the treatment at Emory would help, and then I prayed that the new treatment at the National Cancer Institute would do some good. But all the while, I was afraid these treatments would weaken Billy so much that he couldn't enjoy whatever time he had left.

But I always left the decision about treatment up to him. I knew after living with Billy for more than 30 years that I was not going to change his mind once he'd made a decision.

It's strange, though, even when I knew the end was near, I didn't feel like Billy's life was over. I thought his final statement would be in the way he died—full of life and hope and caring until the very end.

I saw Billy change and grow in ways I would have never thought possible. He saw so much more meaning in life than he had ever seen before. His determination and will had always been there, but he was amazing in the last year of his life. He just wouldn't quit. I think everyone who came into contact with him could sense his courage and will, and the strength his sobriety gave to him.

* * *

I was more than willing to be Billy's nurse, chauffeur and nutritionist after he became ill. But I tried not to coddle him.

All I tried to do was make sure he didn't tire himself out. Once Billy got going, he didn't want to stop, and he'd never tell anybody he was too tired to do something.

He'd be exhausted when we got home from one of his out-of-town speaking engagements. But he wouldn't have had it any other way. He loved being around people and the media, and talking about his recovery from alcoholism.

In the last year, he began to realize how important it was for him to share his story about alcoholism. Before, I don't think he thought anyone cared.

I would get bone tired, too. At times, I just functioned on automatic pilot. But I always knew that I could rest later.

* * *

Billy always accused me of tagging along with him on his speeches so he wouldn't say anything bad about me.

I told him he had it all wrong. I needed to be there to tell people what it was really like when he was drinking.

Billy and I spoke together for CareUnit five times during the last year of his life and did a lot of television, radio and newspaper interviews together. And, like I said, Billy never ceased to amaze me. He improved each time he spoke.

In the beginning, he never prepared for a speech. He would just get up, say a few words, and answer questions from the audience. He was always funny, but he had no real coherent message. It seemed like half the questions he answered would be about Jimmy, Libya or Billy Beer.

Gradually, though, he began making notes in secret and asking for critiques of his performance from his friends. The next thing I knew, he had improved 100 percent. I guess he didn't need my help as much as I thought he did.

In his last speech in Tampa, he wasn't asked a single question about Jimmy or about Libya. It was as if he had finally come out from under Jimmy's shadow after all these years.

* * *

Through Billy, I have been able to carve out a career of sorts as a consultant and speaker on family issues surrounding alcoholism. I have done some work for Union Pacific and Burlington Northern on their family assistance programs and try to speak as often as I can.

I still feel my first responsibility is to my family, but Billy and my friends have encouraged me to continue speaking. Billy made me promise that I would continue speaking after he was gone.

A lot of people think I'm strong, but I'm really a very emotional person. I know that I'll start crying like a baby the first time I speak again.

I substituted for Billy as a speaker at CareUnit Hospital of St. Louis while Billy was in the hospital at Emory, and I broke up several times while I was speaking. The comforting thing, though, was that everyone in the audience cried along with me.

The very first time I was asked to speak, I was so nervous that I didn't think I could go through with it. Fortunately, Billy was there to support me, and the audience seemed to relate well to what I was saying. That gave me a little confidence.

Billy was always nervous before he spoke, but he wouldn't admit it to a soul, not even me. I could sense his nervousness through his mannerisms and his pattern of speaking. He fidgeted with his hands when he was nervous and stammered at times.

Throughout our life together, I always wished Billy had had more self-confidence. Toward the end, I think he did. He had finally discovered the strength of his convictions.

* * *

My message is that alcoholism is a family disease and that the family members of an alcoholic need treatment, too.

I'm a member of Al-Anon, a self-help group for people who live with alcoholics. We're the ones who used to try to control and protect our alcoholics and couldn't understand why they didn't appreciate what we were doing for them.

Billy always chided me about being a member of Al-Anon and used to claim that Al-Anons were plotting to take over all the A.A. meetings in the world. But I think he loved Al-Anon. It gave him something to complain about.

I underwent three weeks of treatment in a family program at Long Beach Naval Hospital, while Billy was in treatment. Those three weeks changed my life.

I went to Long Beach with Billy with the intention of dropping him off and going back home. My attitude was:

"He's all yours, now. Fix him, and send him home to me when he's fixed."

But Dr. Pursch (Capt. Joseph Pursch, chief of the Navy's Alcohol Rehabilitation Program at the time) set me straight. He told me that I needed help, too, and he asked me how I felt. That floored me. I don't think anybody had ever asked me how I felt before.

During treatment, I learned that I had to pull away and let Billy take responsibility for his own life.

It was hard to let go, but I did and found a new independence. This last year would have been unbearable if I hadn't changed.

* * *

A lot of our friends don't understand these changes. They think I deserve praise for putting up with all of Billy's nonsense when he was drinking.

They don't realize that I was a convenient doormat for Billy.

Frances Irlbeck, Billy's former secretary, says Billy could never have gotten along without me. She says Billy always depended on me to get his butt out of a crack.

Nookie Meadows (a Georgia State Legislator and automobile dealer who, according to Billy, has never said an unkind word about anyone), told me he really didn't see how I stayed with Billy all those years. He said I was the backbone of Billy.

And our son-in-law Mark Fuller, who traveled with Billy for two years when he was on the celebrity tour during Jimmy's term of office, says there would be no Carter family if I hadn't kept everything together.

A few years ago, Mark told me: "Miss Sybil, I think Mr. Billy would be dead now if it hadn't been for you."

Everyone is mostly right, but that's not something I'm proud of.

I didn't set out to be a martyr, but I acted like one. I was constantly trying to save someone's feelings—the children's, Billy's, Miss Lillian's. Everyone's feelings except my own.

I realize now people were looking at me, saying, "Poor Sybil." They were pitying me for what I put up with, and I hated it. I'm not that way any longer, thank God.

* * *

After all the pain we'd been through because of drinking, our marriage almost ended in Billy's first year of sobriety.

Our life was a mess when Billy came home from Long Beach. Billy's income from personal appearances had dried up overnight because of his connection with the Libyan government, the Internal Revenue Service was investigating us, Billy was under subpoena to testify at two hearings concerning campaign contributions, and the Libyan affair, which the press called "Billygate," was about to blow up.

On top of all this, Billy and I were trying to iron things out in our relationship.

It was almost like we were starting over again. I felt a little lost and frightened and knew I was going to have to fight for everything I wanted and needed. If anything, I was crazier than I had been when Billy was drinking. How was I going to be a good mother and a good wife without losing my independence?

I probably overcompensated, but I was determined not to revert to my old ways. I called Billy's hand on everything, and he withdrew from me. We weren't close at all, but it didn't bother me at the time because I knew we were both making a lot of adjustments.

Then in June of 1980, I found out Billy was having an affair with a woman in Atlanta. It almost killed me.

* * *

I truly hated Billy when I found out what was going on. After putting up with all of his nonsense, I felt betrayed and used. I felt that he didn't love me the way I loved him. The hurt was so great that I wished I were dead.

I never did like it when he was running around the country with Miss Peanut Lolita and other girls at promotional events. I knew he didn't want me with him, but deep in my heart, I thought I could trust him.

Billy told me he wanted a divorce, but that he wanted me to file for it.

I told him I wouldn't. If he wanted a divorce, he had to file himself.

* * *

Some of our kids have asked why on earth we would want to bring up Billy's affair. We told them that it is part of our story and that we wanted our story to be an honest one.

I think it's something Billy would rather have forgotten, too. But he knew we had to deal with it.

Billy told me later that he was all screwed up at the time and that he didn't like the way things were going at home. He said he was ready to take charge of the family and that I wasn't ready to give up control. He said he didn't like that at all.

Billy later admitted he had made a mistake, but said he didn't think I would ever forgive him.

I surprised him. I told him I would forgive him, but I never would forget, and I didn't think he would either.

We all make mistakes and without forgiveness where would any of us be.

It wasn't in Billy's nature to say he was sorry for what happened. He always just kind of assumed that you knew he was sorry for something he had done and that he would try to make up for it in other ways.

* * *

I didn't make things easy for Billy about the affair. I insisted that he tell the children that he wanted a divorce. I wouldn't do it for him. I had learned in treatment to make him take responsibility for his actions.

Jana told me that she and Kim were at the service station when he arrived at about 10 o'clock at night to tell them that he and I were getting a divorce.

Jana said one of the first things that entered her mind was: "I bet Mama made him tell us."

Our children knew us pretty well.

The other children found out at our home in Buena Vista (north of Plains). I think it hit Buddy hardest of all. He lost a lot of respect for his father, and it took him a long time to get it back.

Marle was the last to hear.

Marle walked into the living room and saw all of us sitting around with our heads hanging down. She told me later that she thought somebody had died. Buddy and Mandy were there, and I was holding Earl in my arms. Finally, Billy looked up and blurted, "Marle, your Mama and I are getting a divorce."

If it hadn't been so sad, it would have been comical. Marle was shocked, but I don't think she or the other children ever thought we would go through with it.

Kim told me that she had heard us talk about getting a divorce before when Billy was drinking, so she never did take the whole thing too seriously.

I also made Billy tell Jimmy and Miss Lillian.

Miss Lillian never mentioned it to me, but Jimmy told Billy, "If you go ahead with this, you will be making the biggest mistake of your life."

I don't know when the affair ended, but Billy never did mention it or a divorce again.

* * *

While Billy was ill, we tried to keep everything operating as normally as possible. That was better for everyone, particularly Earl and the grandchildren.

Billy helped me keep up with my gardening, and we redecorated the house. The redecorating, though, was mostly my project. All Billy cared about was his easy chair in front of the television. When he was home, he stayed plopped in that chair, reading, watching sports and carrying on conversations with everybody in the room. I don't know how he did it, but he could talk and watch TV at the same time and never miss a beat.

* * *

One thing I'll never change in our home are the pictures on the walls. In our den and living room, we've got lots of photos of Billy and his friends during those crazy days when Jimmy was president.

But maybe my proudest possession is the full-length portrait of Miss Lillian, which hangs in the hallway.

Miss Lillian willed the portrait to me, and I feel so close to her when I look at it.

I always felt more like a daughter than a daughter-in-law to her.

She said I was the only common sense person in the whole family. Billy and Miss Lillian were very close, but my relationship to her was always different.

I was impressed with Miss Lillian's strength and her unconditional support of Billy and her other children.

I always bristle at the stereotype of Southern women as weak-willed and subservient. Miss Lillian was anything but subservient. She was the strength of the Carter family. She did what she wanted, and she encouraged each of her children to do the same. I never heard Miss Lillian criticize Billy for anything he did—no matter how outrageous it might have been. She was very strong and very tolerant. Not at all a Southern Belle.

I hope that people look at me the same way.

CHAPTER FIVE

Billy

Ever since my public life began with Jimmy's election to the presidency, I've been asked over and over if Jimmy and I were as different as we seem.

That's like asking me if the Pope is Catholic. Jimmy and I aren't a bit alike.

We're closer now, but we're as different as night and day.

Jimmy's thirteen years older than me, and we really never spent much time under the same roof. He went off to college and the Navy and didn't return home until Daddy died in 1953. By then I was 16, and pretty much my own person.

A lot of people think that my drinking and hell-raising were the result of having a famous brother. All I can say is: no way. I was drinking and raising hell long before Jimmy became famous.

Mama and Daddy never held up Jimmy's accomplishments to me. We're not like the Roosevelts or Kennedys or some other high-achieving family.

The most serious problem Jimmy and I ever had was over the family peanut business. I thought I should have been allowed to buy him out after he was elected president, but his advisors wanted him to put it into a blind trust.

That left me without any roots, and I resented it. And I resented Jimmy for letting it happen.

But it sure as hell didn't make me what I am. I take full responsibility for that.

* * *

If anything, I may be a little more restrained around Jimmy than I am with my close friends. That stands to reason. I never went out drinking or raising hell with Jimmy. And we never sat around together telling lies like I do with Hogpen Johnson or some of my other cronies.

But still our relationship is pretty informal.

Since we moved back to Plains, we visit almost every day when we're both in town. Jimmy will come over to borrow my weed-eater, or to watch a baseball game on television or something.

When Rosalynn's not at home, Jimmy usually comes around at dinner or supper time. He likes Sybil's cooking. He enjoys the collard greens and sweets she cooks. I think he gets tired of all that health food he and Rosalynn eat.

I don't visit Jimmy too often. He's got a need for privacy, and I respect that.

I'm much more visible around Plains than Jimmy, and you'd be surprised how many tourists ask me right out of the blue if I could take them to visit Jimmy.

One day this real pretty young girl came up to me while I was cutting the grass along our fence and told me she'd give me anything I wanted if I would introduce her to Jimmy.

I told Jimmy if she ever came back, he might expect a visitor. I said I would wait until Rosalynn was gone before I brought her around.

* * *

Jimmy and I live next to each other, with the Secret Service compound in between. There's a pond in front of Jimmy's house where Earl and I go to feed the fish.

Jimmy mows the grass around the pond, which is one reason he stays so fit. He's pretty trim for a person his age (64). He keeps his weight about 155.

I tell people that Jimmy looks pretty good for a 75 year old man. He comes back with something like, "I look a good sight better than you, and you're only 51."

I like to rag Jimmy about being so competitive. I'm competitive, too, so it's fair game.

Those softball games we had while he was president were real bloodbaths. My team was made up of media guys and Jimmy's was made up of Secret Service agents—and the umpires. We didn't have one call go in our favor the whole time we played.

We'd also bring in ringers from time to time. Once we conned one of the networks into reassigning this former ballplayer to Plains just to help us win. But it didn't help. Jimmy had his pick of the agents and the umpires.

One time I got so mad when the umpire called Jimmy safe at first that I threw the ball at Jimmy. And he just stood there on first base looking smug and self-righteous. If it hadn't been for the Secret Service agents, I would have killed him.

CHAPTER FIVE

Another time, Buck Sappenfield, a friend of mine, grabbed Jimmy from behind in a bear hug at first base, and you would have thought World War III had broken out. Secret Service agents came running from everywhere.

I just stood on the mound and laughed while poor Buck about got wasted.

I was telling all this stuff to a psychiatrist at Long Beach Naval Hospital when I was in treatment, and he sat there nodding his head like he had just found the clue to why I was such a maniac.

I told him that was nothing. All of us Carters were that way. I would have taken the last dime off my best friend in a poker or crap game. In fact, I once won a Corvette from a guy shooting craps at my service station.

I tooled around Plains in that Corvette for a couple of years until I finally sold it for $6,000.

* * *

Jimmy says I am more like Mama, or Gloria, or Ruth than I am him. He's probably right.

Not long ago a friend of mine asked Jimmy how he thought we were different, and you'd thought Jimmy was reciting from "The Book of Lists."

Here's what Jimmy said:

— "I've always been envious of Billy's ability to gather people around him and have fun. I can't do that.

— Billy's had this element of irresponsibility—that he didn't give a damn—that I find intriguing. Nothing would grieve me more than to be thought of as irresponsible."

— "I always set specific goals for myself; Billy did not."

— "I'm highly disciplined; Billy is not."

— "I'm always well prepared for any task I undertake; Billy is not."

— "There's absolutely nothing unorthodox about me; Billy's always been unorthodox."

— "I'm deeply religious. Even devout. Billy's not."

— "I'm reconciliatory by nature; Billy's not."

— "I'm very circumspect in what I say and do; Billy's not."

I think you get the point. Jimmy thinks we're not much alike.

* * *

Jimmy Carter

Despite the differences between his brother and him, former President Carter warns that people should exercise caution in analyzing Billy.

"Much of what Billy says or does belies his inner competence. He could play the country bumpkin as well as anyone. His beer drinking helped promote that image. He had a can of beer in his hand in every photo I ever saw of him during the first part of my presidency.

"Billy's extremely intelligent. His incisiveness and his wit made him a good match for the newspeople who interviewed him. I think the reporters and newscasters who really got to know Billy enjoyed him and recognized his intelligence.

"Mother once said that Billy was the most intelligent of her children. I don't think I would quarrel with that. Before I decided to enter politics, Billy was better versed than I was in national and international affairs. I had more of a narrow focus and had been concentrating almost exclusively on state agricultural affairs and on ways to improve our peanut business.

"Billy is basically a self-taught person. He's a voracious reader and has remarkable powers of retention. All of us children turned out to be readers. I believe Mother engendered that in us.

"I was disappointed that Billy didn't take advantage of his intellect to finish college, but Billy's native intelligence and his skills in dealing with people have more than compensated for his lack of formal education."

* * *

I never get tired of telling the story that Mama said I was the smartest one in the family. I always said Mama was a very perceptive woman.

I think one of the biggest differences between Jimmy and me—other than his accomplishments—is that Jimmy's very intense and has more of a one track mind than I do.

I've always gone off in a million different directions and like to have a good time. Jimmy goes after something all the way until he gets it done.

I never would have guessed that he would be president one day, but when he told me he was running for it, I didn't have the slightest doubt that he would give it all he had and that he just might pull it off.

CHAPTER FIVE

My sister Gloria said all four of us kids were pretty smart, but the main difference between us was that Jimmy and Ruth were ambitious, as well as smart.

No one could ever accuse Gloria of being ambitious. She stayed out of the limelight while Jimmy was president, and it didn't bother her a bit. I think the thing she's proudest of in her life was being named to the *Easy Rider* magazine "Hall of Fame."

* * *

Jimmy still believes that my alcoholism was, in some way, related to his rise in politics.

Sybil and I both told him that my problems with drinking started way before he was elected governor.

But Jimmy can be stubborn, too. He just won't accept what we say. I told Sybil she ought to cart Jimmy off to an Al-Anon meeting. Maybe he and Gerald Ford could start up a meeting.

Sybil asked Jimmy to talk with me a couple of times about my drinking. But, truthfully, he had a better chance of getting the hostages out of Iran than he had in getting me to stop drinking.

Both times I told him, "Hell, Jimmy, I'll watch it. I'm just out drinking with the boys. I can't take Sybil with me to the places I go."

Jimmy said he probably could have done more if he hadn't been so ignorant about alcoholism.

I told him he couldn't have done a thing. The only people who really know about alcoholism are other alcoholics.

As good as Dr. Pursch was in treating me for my alcoholism, he could never get through to me like another alcoholic.

* * *

Jimmy Carter knew that from the time Billy returned to Plains following his discharge from the Marines that his younger brother loved to drink and carouse with his friends after work and on weekends.

"Right after work, he'd hit Joe Bacon's club on the outskirts of town. That wasn't a place for the faint-hearted. He was frequently out all weekend with his friends. He wasn't being attentive to Sybil or his family. But still it never occurred to me that he was an alcoholic."

"My perception of an alcoholic was that of a person who couldn't hold a job or provide for himself or his family. It was an honest perception. Two of my mother's brothers, Jack and Lem Gordy, were problem drinkers, and Jack eventually died in the Anchorage, a home for alcoholics (in Albany, Geor-

gia). Uncle Lem, though, quit drinking and had been sober 12 years when he died.

"Several times, either my mother or grandmother would ask me to go find Uncle Jack and take him to the Anchorage. I would usually find Uncle Jack in jail. It was sad.

"Billy didn't fit that stereotype.

"He would always be back at work on Monday regaling everyone with his stories about how he had gotten into a fight at some bar or honky tonk. To my knowledge, he never won a fight. All I ever heard was him talking about getting his face smashed in, or getting thrown out of a bar. This was all part of Billy's charm. People responded to him and to his self-deprecating stories and humor."

* * *

"I am proud of how Billy dealt first with his alcoholism and then his cancer.

"I think Billy has been an inspiration to hundreds, or maybe even thousands of people. He and Sybil worked hard to spread the message about alcoholism. I know that I, for one, have learned a lot from them. I believe Billy's recovery from alcoholism was his proudest achievement, and that it enabled him to become what he was in the last year of his life.

"Billy's reaction to cancer was nothing short of amazing. He was able to accommodate cancer with a generosity and humor that would be difficult for anyone to match. He chose to make the most of his life in his last 13 months. He was interested in helping other people and in enjoying his own family to the fullest. Sometimes when we're faced with great illness, our true character comes out. I believe that happened with Billy. He was triumphant over tragedy.

"I learned to appreciate him more and more, and I think many other people did, too. He became a legitimately popular figure on his own, quite apart from me. Certainly, his success as a person was no longer dependent on his relationship with me—not that it ever really was."

* * *

Even though Jimmy and I weren't really close until recently, I always knew he cared about me.

I used to joke that the only reason Jimmy didn't kick my ass was that he was afraid Mama would kick his if he did.

He should have disowned me about the Libyan thing, but he didn't. I still don't think I should have been required to register as a foreign agent. When that happened, I stormed to the White House to give Jimmy hell about it, but his aides wouldn't let me see him. He was on the tennis court at the time, and they practically had to hog-tie me to keep me from going out there. Jimmy's lawyers had advised him not to communicate with me until the Senate hearing on the Libyan matter was over, and he never violated that.

A couple of his advisers wanted Jimmy to come down hard on me publicly, but Jimmy ignored them, even though I know he was mad as hell at me. A friend of mine told me he had never heard Jimmy cuss like he did when he found out I was going to Libya the first time. I think his advisers favored deporting me to Libya.

* * *

I don't think I've ever told Jimmy this, but I'm proud that he was elected president and think he's borne up well against a lot of criticism.

I'm not going to tell you that I think Jimmy was a great president. I think Harry Truman was the only great president in my lifetime. But I believe he did a lot better job than everyone gives him credit for. He had some good theories on human rights and putting government back in the hands of the people. And he was honest, which is damned near impossible to be in politics. In my opinion, the longer someone's in politics, the dirtier he gets.

But I really don't think Jimmy had a chance in hell to succeed. He was a Southerner and an outsider to Washington, and the Northern press still thinks we lynch blacks, wear overalls and go barefooted down here. People like William Safire (of the New York Times) were just lying back waiting to crucify Jimmy the first time he messed up.

If Jimmy had done some of the things Reagan has done, they would have wanted to impeach him.

I've sometimes wondered what life would have been like if Jimmy had been reelected in 1980. But I try not to think about it too much. Four years might not have been enough for Jimmy, but it was enough for me.

CHAPTER SIX

Frances Irlbeck is a small, but strong-willed, 46 year old widowed mother of four with large blue eyes. Today, she works long hours in the kitchen of the Kountry Korner Restaurant in Plains, across the street and railroad tracks from the former Carter peanut warehouse, where she took a job in 1960 as a peanut sheller.

She is an unabashed admirer of Billy Carter, for whom she worked in the warehouse and later as his private secretary. "I like Jimmy Carter, but I love Billy Carter." she says.

Recently, Frances sat at a table with a red-and-white checkered tablecloth in the Kountry Korner, sipping coffee, smoking cigarettes and reminiscing about her former boss. During the course of her conversation, she suddenly paused and said wistfully.

"You know. I just can't imagine Plains, Georgia, without Billy Carter."

* * *

While most of the nation associates this serene southwestern Georgia farming community of 680 with the former president, the townspeople seem to associate it more closely with Billy, even though he only recently moved back to Plains after an absence of 10 years.

"Really, it never seemed like Billy lived anywhere else," says Gloria Spann, Billy's older sister, who, like Frances Irlbeck, has lived in Plains her entire life.

"Billy's heart has always been in Plains. Unlike Jimmy, Billy's friends are here, and his and Sybil's children and grandchildren are here," says Gloria, an energetic woman who scoots around the country on a thunderous Harley Davidson motorcycle and lives with her husband Walter on a farm on the southern outskirts of town.

"When we were kids," she continues, "Jimmy wanted to be an admiral and Ruth (who was three years younger than Gloria) wanted to be a celebrity. But Billy and I wanted to stay home. I wanted to be a farmer's wife, which I am, and Billy wanted to run Daddy's business, the peanut warehouse. He wasn't able to do that after Jimmy was elected president."

* * *

Things went crazy in Plains when Jimmy was elected president, and Sybil, the kids and I had to move to get some privacy. Simple as that.

We moved up near Buena Vista, about 30 miles north. Our place was so secluded that even our friends got lost trying to find it. Georgia has so many back roads that if you don't know what you're doing, you'll end up going in circles.

At times, I was so drunk that I got lost trying to find our house. At least, that's what I used to tell Sybil when I dragged in at 2 or 3 in the morning. Once I told Sybil I was late because I got caught in traffic while a circus was setting up in town. I told her it took forever for the elephants to cross the road.

She just looked at me and said, "Bull." I thought she would at least laugh.

Another advantage of the place in Buena Vista was that it was set way back on 60 acres of land and wasn't accessible on foot.

There were 20,000 tourists a day pouring into Plains right after Jimmy's election. Cars would be bumper-to-bumper for about 10 miles, from Americus to Plains. Highway 280 looked like a Los Angeles freeway.

With all those people around, plus the media, there was no place for Sybil, the kids or me to hide. We were usually the only Carters around. Mama spent most of her time out at the pond house west of town, which is set back off the main road in the woods. And Gloria became damned near invisible. She dropped the "Carter" from Gloria Carter Spann during that time.

I continued to work at the warehouse for a while after we moved, and I held on to the gas station until 1981. I also set up my "press headquarters" at the Best Western Motel in Americus. Jimmy Murray had a good bar there, and I could have a few beers with my breakfast.

We lived in Buena Vista seven years before moving to Waycross, Georgia, about 150 miles to the east of Plains, where I worked with a mobile home manufacturing company for three years.

In 1987, an opportunity came along with Ocilla Industries at their modular home plant in Arabi, about 50 miles south of Plains, and we decided to move back home. I had to commute about 100 miles round-trip to work, but that didn't bother me. I used to drive a couple of hundred miles a day on the back roads on the weekends in my pickup, drinking beer and talking with the people on the way.

People reminded me that back in the 70s I had said I would never live in Plains again. Hell, I didn't mean half what I said back then, and the other half I didn't remember. Anyway, we wanted to come back home.

* * *

Plains hasn't changed a lot since I was a boy growing up here.

Most of the junk businesses that sprang up when Jimmy was president are gone now. Our cousin, Hugh Carter, still sells some stuff at his antique store downtown, including empty cans of Billy Beer.

I've only got three six-packs of unopened cans of Billy Beer left. I can't believe it, but collectors are willing to pay about $500 for a six-pack of Billy Beer. I always said you had to be an alcoholic to drink Billy Beer.

It was terrible.

Plains is kind of a pretty little town. Most of the 1920 white frame houses along Church Street, our main street, were spruced up while Jimmy was president and are kept up real well. What I like most, though, are the trees, giant oaks, pecans and pines. The property values in Plains went wild for a while when Jimmy was president.

Some people lost a lot of money, but it served them right. Most of them were out-of-town speculators, and they were driving up prices for people who had lived here all their lives.

Not too long ago, one of our friends, Doug Unger, bought an old house on Church Street for about half what some woman from Texas had paid for it. And she had spent a small fortune restoring it.

So I guess us rednecks won out in the end.

* * *

After Jimmy was elected, I went to visit Lady Bird Johnson to see how they had coped with the tourist problem in Johnson City, Texas, which was about the same size as Plains. But they never had the problems we did. Johnson City was more off the beaten track than Plains. We had tourists coming through Georgia from the North and Midwest on their way to Florida. Also, Johnson lived out of town on a ranch—not in town like Jimmy did.

More than anything, though, I think the press painted this picture of Plains as one of those Norman Rockwell-like small towns, full of colorful characters, and people became fascinated with the place.

I wanted to keep the town like it was, but a lot of people wanted to profit from the tourism. There was one plan to sell one-inch-square blocks of land in Plains for something like $5 a square. The profits off that deal would have been about a million dollars. Jimmy asked me if I could put a stop to that deal, and I did. But it caused a lot of hard feelings.

Gloria got mad at me about this time, and we didn't speak to each for the next eight years. She thought I was profiting more off Jimmy's election than anyone else in Plains and said I ought to mind my own business.

One day there was a funeral in town, and a reporter asked me if I liked going to funerals. I told him the only funeral I was looking forward to was Gloria's.

I regretted saying that later, but since Gloria and I weren't speaking, I couldn't apologize to her.

* * *

Carter family homes are all over town and the countryside outside of town. Today, the older homes have historical markers on the street in front of them. Mama and Daddy's home, where we moved when I was about 12, has been converted into an office for Jimmy, and our two eldest daughters, Kim and Jana and their families live within a block of each other on the north edge of Plains, not far from our old house on Bond Street, where we lived for 15 years before moving to Buena Vista.

My old two-pump service station is on Church Street across from downtown. The downtown buildings are mostly deserted now. About the only buildings still in use are Hugh Carter's antique store and his Carter Worm Farm Office.

Kitty-corner from downtown and my old service station is our peanut warehouse. You can still see a "Carter Warehouse" sign near the top of the main warehouse. Our property was more than just a warehouse. There's a shelling plant, a couple of warehouses, a cotton gin, a laboratory, scales and the like. They sit on 22 acres of land.

It's called Golden Peanut Company now. They are a subsidiary of a big Midwestern agricultural conglomerate. In 1987, when the main office in the Midwest considered shutting down the old plant and consolidating their Georgia operations, Jimmy flew to the company headquarters to persuade them to keep the warehouse open.

They finally decided to keep it open.

When I was a kid growing up, I thought I would be running that warehouse 'til the day I died. I didn't know what a conglomerate was. All I knew was that it was Daddy's warehouse, and by God, someday I was going to run it.

* * *

In May of 1988, I took a friend to visit the warehouse. It was the first time I had been in the yard since I left the peanut business in 1977.

Peanut harvest was still three or four months away, and the yard was almost empty.

I hadn't avoided the yard on purpose, but I didn't see any point in hanging around there.

While I was visiting, I ran into Clarence Welch, who used to work with Jimmy and me and still works there.

Clarence told me things were fine at the warehouse, but said they'd never be the same as when we ran it.

I said, "Remember how full the yard used to be during the peak season, Clarence? You could hardly make your way around the wagons. We had about a thousand tons of unloaded peanuts at any given time. We just couldn't keep up."

"Yeh," Clarence said. "We worked hard, but it was fun. We were like a family."

Clarence and I used to work together in the cotton gin on the back of the property, and we hated it. We'd get all that damned dust and lint up our noses and complain like hell.

I remember Clarence being all dusty and grimy, and looking up at me and saying, "What are we doing in this damned cotton gin. We're peanut men."

* * *

Clarence Welch has worked at the peanut warehouse for a number of years for the Carters—both Jimmy and Billy—and for the firms that succeeded the Carters.

He says flatly that Billy was the best boss he ever had.

"Billy and Sybil looked after us. They worked side by side with us, seven

days a week during harvest. We really miss them. The biggest mistake Billy ever made was leaving the peanut business. It was part of him."

* * *

Frank McGarragh, a 54 year old black, began working at the warehouse for the Carters in 1960 as an equipment operator. Today, he works at the University of Georgia agricultural experiment station east of Plains.

"I'd still be at the warehouse if Billy was running it," Frank says. "We were like a team. The Carters treated everyone the same—blacks, whites, rich and poor.

"Billy was always himself. He was never too busy to take time with you. I'm glad he and Sybil came back to Plains. He'll always be one of my best friends."

* * *

Sybil says those days at the warehouse were the happiest times of her life. We worked hard, but we worked together as a family, and times were really good.

I drank in those days, too, but I never drank on the job, and I never shirked my duties.

While I managed the warehouse, I worked 12 hours a day and drank four hours. After I left the warehouse and started doing promotions, I worked four hours and drank 12. It was one of those mid-career changes. I became a professional drinker.

* * *

I left the business in 1977 after it was put into a blind trust following Jimmy's election. I wanted to buy the business, but Charles Kirbo (the Atlanta attorney who managed the trust) turned down my offer. At the time, I owned about one-sixth of the business, and Jimmy and Mama owned the remaining five-sixths.

Kirbo asked me to stay on, but I told him I'd rather fry in hell.

* * *

Gloria and most of Billy's friends and family think that Billy should have had the opportunity to take over the business.

Gloria says, "If I were Billy, I would be resentful, too. Jimmy wasn't around much and wasn't that involved in the business. I think Jimmy should have trusted Billy more than he did Kirbo."

CHAPTER SIX

Family friend, Randy Coleman, who worked at the warehouse for both Jimmy and Billy, says:

"The last year Billy ran the warehouse, we bought 22,000 tons of peanuts. The first year Kirbo ran it, they didn't buy a tenth of that. Only about 1500 tons. Now, you tell me, who was right."

* * *

To this day, Jimmy Carter defends Charles Kirbo's decision. "I'm sorry Billy feels as he does about Charles Kirbo. Kirbo is the best friend I've ever had, and I have complete trust in him.

"Billy felt as though he was capable of running the business successfully, but I have serious doubts about that. Billy became infatuated with celebrity and was spending more and more time on the road, appearing on "Hee-Haw" and the like. He was also drinking too much, in my opinion. Besides, the warehouse was losing money. Kirbo simply decided that Billy wasn't getting things done, and I supported that decision.

"I doubt Billy and I will ever resolve our disagreement on the Kirbo matter. We haven't discussed the matter in years."

* * *

I would expect Jimmy to defend Kirbo. I don't see it the way he does, and never will. We weren't losing money until Kirbo took over.

Some friends of mine thought I should have tried to get back in the business a few years ago. But the business has changed. It's not just you and the farmers any longer.

Sometimes, though, I do wonder what it would have been like to have remained at the warehouse. But I don't think about it often. I don't have the desire or the ambition to get back into the business.

It's too damned much work.

Hogpen Johnson and I are looking for a business where we won't have to work too hard. We've got our eye on the Busy Bee cab company in Americus. They've got one cab and no customers as far as we can tell. That's my kind of business.

CHAPTER SEVEN

When Daddy died in 1953 and Jimmy returned from the Navy to run the warehouse, I kissed my chances of managing the business goodbye.

And, even though, I was just 16, I was mad as hell. I didn't think that's what Daddy would have wanted.

I thought Mama should run the business with my help until I was old enough to take over. I was already bad stubborn and didn't want to take orders from anybody, including Jimmy.

I was a lot closer to Daddy than Mama while I was growing up.

I loved Mama, but we didn't become real close until I returned to Plains after getting out of the Marines. I wanted to be just like Daddy, but really I guess I was a lot like Mama all along. I always said exactly what was on my mind, just like Mama. Daddy was a good sight more diplomatic.

I wanted to be with Daddy all the time.

One of my earliest memories is going with Daddy to the Elk's Club and playing the horse racing machine while Daddy was playing poker with his friends. Man, I thought that's the way life ought to be. Daddy worked hard—and he made me work hard—but he also liked to have a good time. The best I remember is most everybody liked Daddy. I never heard anyone speak bad about him.

I also liked being out with Daddy in the fields near our house. Daddy wasn't doing much of the actual farming in 1937, when I was born, but he knew every inch of our land. He had been farming in Archery, about three miles west of Plains, since the 1920s, and had opened the warehouse a few years later. He also had an insurance business at one time.

* * *

Gloria says, "Billy was with Daddy an awful lot. I think Daddy felt that he had done the best he could with Jimmy, Ruth and me. Now, he was just going to enjoy Billy."

In 1978, Billy's late sister Ruth recalled in her book, Brother Billy, *that as a child Billy would walk the peanut fields with his father near their large frame house in Archery outside of Plains, and that Mr. Earl would patiently explain how the peanuts grew and matured beneath the red Georgia soil.*

"Billy loved it," Ruth said, "because it was Daddy's world. Billy (became) a confirmed son of the soil, and always would be."

* * *

Daddy was elected to the State Legislature one year before he died, and I worked as a page in the Legislature during the winter of 1953.

That was one of the best times of my life. Just the two of us living together in Atlanta. Mostly, I remember us talking a lot. He was real patient with me, and I really felt a part of everything he was doing.

There was no way for me to know what was just around the corner. Daddy got sick a little bit later, and the doctors treated him for everything, but nothing worked. They didn't realize he had cancer. By the time, he went to Atlanta for surgery, it was too late.

After the doctors sent him home, I was with him a lot. He never said a word about dying, and I didn't either.

* * *

Iced tea in hand, Jimmy Carter, the nation's 39th president, leaned back on the couch in the den of his home a few hundred yards from Billy's home on Church Street and reflected on his younger brother's early years and the effect their father's death in 1953 had on Billy.

"I never tried to assume a fatherly role in Billy's life after Daddy died. Billy was very close to Daddy. I could never have been a replacement for Daddy in Billy's eyes even if I had wanted to be.

"It was almost preordained that one day Daddy would turn the peanut business over to Billy. No one ever questioned that. I was very happy in the Navy, and neither Mama nor my sisters had any strong interest in managing the business.

"Sadly, two things happened which must have been a great shock to Billy. Daddy died prematurely when Billy was only 16, and Mama asked me to come back to Plains to run the business.

"Billy was only three years old when I left for college, so we had never spent much time together. I really didn't know Billy very well at the time Daddy died, but I feel that he resented my coming back to run the business because he had thought it would be his one day. Also, he was deeply hurt that Daddy had died and left him. He ended up lashing out at the situation. Things just hadn't worked out the way he or any of us had planned."

* * *

CHAPTER SEVEN

Gloria recalled:

"Everything was a mess when Daddy died. Mama was very depressed and wasn't able to be of much help to Billy. In fact, we finally encouraged her to take a trip to Canada for awhile for a change of scenery.

"I also think Billy was resentful of Jimmy's coming back. The way Billy looked at it, it was his warehouse and his job, and here was Jimmy giving him orders and so on. I can understand why he was resentful.

"I remember on the night we discovered that Daddy was terminally ill, we stayed overnight in a boarding house near Emory University Hospital. That night everyone was sitting around very quietly. Suddenly, someone—I don't remember who—killed a bug in the room. Billy went into hysterics over the death of that bug. It was frightening. I guess he was reacting to everything that was going on. Daddy's illness was hard on everyone, but it was particularly hard on Billy."

* * *

Finally, I decided to hell with it. Let Jimmy run the warehouse. He could do it without me.

I was ready to raise a little hell. I got a little out of control. It got to the point that my friends' mothers didn't want them hanging around with me.

I also said to hell with my schoolwork. I had a running battle with Y.T. Sheffield, the Plains High School Principal. He expelled me several times. But I never did back off.

Daddy was on the Plains School Board and wanted to consolidate the schools in the area. Sheffield opposed that.

My friend Heyward Hobgood, who was a great basketball player, told me that Sheffield pulled him aside one day and told him if he wanted to continue playing basketball, he had better quit hanging around with me. Heyward just ignored him.

I was an A student before Daddy died. After that I just lost interest. I was just biding my time until I graduated from high school and could leave Plains.

It used to make my friend Bud Duvall mad that I could sit in class and read a book while he was studying as hard as he could. I could still make an "A" and Bud would just barely pass.

Mama packed me off to a military school my junior year in high school, and I hated it. But I caused so much trouble there, she decided I couldn't do much worse at home.

I did well enough in high school and on my college entrance exams to be accepted at Emory University in Atlanta. But I decided that could wait. I already had my heart set on joining the Marines.

* * *

I always loved to fight, but I wasn't stupid about it. I was in good shape, but I was only 5-6 and 145 or 150 pounds dripping wet.

So when I picked a fight, I was always sure Bud or Heyward were around. Heyward is six feet nine inches tall and Bud is six feet four and big as a barn. Heyward went on to play college basketball in Kentucky and later toured with the "House of David" professional team.

Once, Heyward, Bud, some other guys and I walked into a large Future Farmers of America meeting in Macon, and I shouted at the top of my lungs:

"We're from Plains, Georgia, and we can whip anybody's butt!"

A lot of people got up and turned around, but they took one look at Heyward and Bud and sat back down.

Most of the stuff we got into wasn't really bad by today's standards—mostly pranks. But I was always doing something. I would do anything, particularly if you dared me to.

Once I pulled off all of my clothes except my underwear and ran about a quarter of a mile through Plains in the cold and ice just to win a dollar bet from Bud and some others. Then somebody said, "I'll bet you two dollars you won't do it buck naked." So, I pulled off my underwear and did it again.

Bud likes to tell about the time he bet me I couldn't eat a plug of chewing tobacco. I tried, but I started turning green and threw up all over the place. Bud said he won, but I said I ate the whole thing before I threw up. I said, hell, I'll do it again just to prove it. He paid up because I don't think he wanted to see me throw up again.

* * *

Mostly what I did was fight. I loved to argue and fight. If you said it was raining, I would say the sun was shining. I would argue with anybody. Most of the time, though, it was just good fun.

Heyward says I'm the only guy who ever called him a son-of-a-bitch and got away with it. I didn't see Heyward much through the years after high school, but when I went to work for Ocilla Industries in Arabi, Heyward was working there as a production foreman. It was like 30 years hadn't passed by. We became real close again.

* * *

Heyward Hobgood, who is now a salesman for Ocilla Industries, says: "Thirty years later, Billy was still the same person he was in high school, even though he'd mellowed out a good bit since he quit drinking. He was still the first person I would go to for advice if I ever had a problem."

* * *

Bud Duvall is a tall heavy-set bachelor who works as a security guard in the Secret Service compound near President Carter's home. He and Billy remained close throughout the years. Bud was one of the regulars at Billy's service station in Plains from 1972 to 1981 when Billy owned the station. He and Billy drank a lot of beer together at the service station, at Mr. Joe's ramshackle beer joint on the outskirts of town, and on the dirt roads around Plains as they drove around in Bud's pick-up truck on lazy weekend days.

"I never thought Billy could stop drinking," Bud says. "Everybody knew he was drinking way too much in the last few years before he quit, but nobody thought he would stop. I sure as hell didn't.

"Billy changed very little over the years. He always said what was on his mind; he always liked to have a good time; and he always liked to hang around with his old friends. He never separated the rich from the poor. He was probably the most honest man I've ever known.

"But, thank God, he quit fighting. I don't think he ever won a fight in his life.

"The last scrape we were in together was at an Americus honky-tonk. Billy got into a argument with somebody, and the next thing I knew there were about 20 of them against three of us.

"I saw that a couple of them had knives, so I slipped across the street to call the cops. When the police arrived, Billy said, 'Who called the cops?' "I said, 'I did,' and Billy got mad as hell at me.

"He said, 'Damn you, Bud, we were doing all right. I don't need any trouble with the police.'"

* * *

I didn't stop fighting until I quit drinking.

I drank beer back when I was a teenager, but really no more or no less than a lot of my friends. I really didn't learn to drink until I was in the Marines.

My reputation for fighting and raising hell always got me in trouble. When anything went on around Plains, they'd come looking for me.

Once somebody blew up the parking lot at the high school, and they tried to blame it on me even though I was out of town at the time.

Years later when Larry Flynt (publisher of *Hustler* magazine) got shot up in Lawrenceville near Atlanta, they investigated me because I had said what a no good, low-down son of a bitch Flynt was. Flynt had started a newspaper in Plains when Jimmy was president, and I was publisher of the other newspaper in town.

Some slime ball that worked for Flynt was always showing up where I was, and I told him if he didn't get out of my face, I was going to kill him.

I had to go through some serious interrogation before I convinced the state police I didn't have anything to do with Flynt's shooting. I told them if I had shot Flynt from 30 feet away, he'd be dead.

I never could understand why Flynt started a paper in Plains. That's how crazy things were.

A lot of people moved into Plains during Jimmy's term. We never knew where most of them came from, why they came, or where they went when they left.

It drove the Secret Service nuts.

* * *

I didn't move from the farm to Plains until 1949, when I was 12. And, believe it or not, I was real shy then—sort of like my son Earl is now.

I really didn't have any friends in Plains, although it was only three miles away. My friends were the black kids from the families who worked for Daddy in Archery.

When I started to school in Plains, I refused to get on the school bus unless my black friend, Bishop Berry, who was two years older, rode on the bus with me.

The Georgia schools were segregated then, but every morning for a few weeks, Bishop would board the bus and ride with me to the Plains elementary school before heading across town on foot to attend the black school.

I also refused to be in our first grade play unless Bishop was in it. So they put in a part for Bishop as a butler to appease me. It was probably the first integrated school play in the South.

* * *

I think one of the reasons I was shy was that I had this persistent stutter, which I've tried hard to overcome. I still lapse into a stutter when I'm real tired, or nervous, or when I'm around somebody else who stutters.

One time, Mel Tillis (a country singer who also stutters) and I were on a radio show together in Georgia. It was awful. We both started stuttering, and neither one of us could get out a word.

Another time, our daughter Marle brought home a friend named Patience, who stuttered real bad. Marle introduced me to Patience, and I started stuttering. Patience thought I was making fun of her until Marle had a chance to explain to her that I stuttered, too.

I later told Patience to just nod at me the next time she visited.

Ruth tells the story in her book about how I began stuttering so bad when I called Mama to tell her Buddy had been born that Mama thought something bad had happened. Mama had to coax all the information out of me bit by bit before she could relax. It must have taken 10 minutes.

* * *

I first met Sybil shortly after she moved to Plains from Eufaula, Alabama, with her parents in 1948.

Sybil was the only girlfriend I ever had. We started going to baseball games together with my parents when I was 13, and things just progressed from there.

I could see Sybil's house from the roof of our garage, and I used to go up there and yell at her. She always accused me of spying on her.

One day in the drugstore, I told Sybil's mama that I wanted to marry Sybil, and Miss Lucille took out a piece of paper and wrote a note promising Sybil to me when we were old enough to get married.

We got married after I finished boot camp in the Marines. I was 18 and Sybil was 16.

Seems like people got married younger back then. You either went to college, joined the military, or got married. I joined the

Marines and got married. Neither one of us had a second thought about getting married so young.

* * *

Jimmy Carter says the family was unhappy with Billy's decision to marry so young.

"We wanted him to wait to get married until he had gone to college. But as it turned out, his decision to marry Sybil was probably the best decision he ever made."

Billy at the lectern at the opening of a new chemical dependency treatment center in Tampa, Florida July 1988. This was his last speaking engagement.

1972

Jimmy and Billy at the shelling plant of Carter's Warehouse in Plains.

1981

Billy and Sybil with their youngest children, Mandy and Earl, on a visit to Circus World in Florida.

DAVID WITBECK

Billy Beer, which was endorsed by Billy and brewed for about a year in 1978 and 1979, has become a collector's item fetching upwards of $500 a six-pack. The beer was an instant sensation when it was introduced by Fall City Brewery of Louisville, Kentucky in 1978, but sales plummeted when the novelty wore off. The beer was also brewed by F.X. Matt Brewery in Utica, New York, Pearl Brewery in Texas, and Cold Springs Brewery in Minnesota. No sales records for the beer are available, but F.X. Matt Brewery noted that it lost money on the venture.

1978

Billy strikes a characteristic pose in front of his famous service station in downtown Plains, which served as his self-proclaimed press headquarters and bar during the early part of Jimmy's presidency. Billy owned the unpretentious two-pump gas station from 1972 to 1981.

1978

LIBYAN GOVERNMENT PHOTO

Billy tours Libyan oil fields in 1978 during the first of his two controversial visits to the North African nation. At far right is Randy Coleman, a long-time friend who acted as Billy's liaison with the Libyan government. Billy's relationship with Libya was highly criticized and resulted in a long Senate investigation.

1978

WHITE HOUSE PHOTO

1978

DALLAS MORNING NEWS

"The Plains Pounder" in the ring with heavyweight champ Joe Frazier.

1985

Billy and Sybil with their children, sons and daughters-in-law, and grandchildren. (l-r) Mandy, Jana, Sybil, Billy, Marle Usry, Jody Usry, Mark Fuller, Kim Fuller, Buddy and his wife, Marlene. (front) Jana's son, Billy; Earl; Kim's daughter, Mandy; Marlene is holding her and Buddy's son, Will.

1977

1978

WHITE HOUSE PHOTO

(l-r) Billy, Ruth, Gloria, Jimmy, and Miss Lillian on the occasion of her 80th birthday, August 15, 1978.

1978

Billy and his agent, Tandy Rice, on the set of *Flatbed Annie and Sweetie Pie,* a 1978 Moonlight Productions film in which Billy played the part of a country sheriff.

1977

Billy and Sybil with Grand Ol' Opry star Minnie Pearl at the Opryland Hotel.

1976

1979

WHITE HOUSE PHOTO

To Billy – with love, Jimmy 2-79

Billy congratulates Jimmy on his receipt of an honorary doctorate from Emory University in Atlanta.

Billy with Tom T. Hall at home between chemotherapy treatments.

BILLY CARTER
1937-1988

"Lord, we pause to wonder if he was the good ol' boy that he was reported to be. He was not always good, and he was the first to admit it. He was not old and never lived to be, and God knows he was not a boy. Billy Carter was a man."

From Tom T. Hall's Eulogy
September 1988

CHAPTER EIGHT

Life in the U.S. Marine Corps agreed with me.

Why not? As a Marine, I could fight, swear, drink and carouse as much as I pleased.

The only problem I had was my vision, which kept me from qualifying for helicopter pilot training, and a commission.

I called a captain a son-of-a-bitch once, but I got off pretty light for that. My real trouble came when I slugged a lieutenant who had shoved me.

I was threatened with a court martial, but a captain I knew bailed me out through one of his old fraternity friends on the review board. The captain hated the lieutenant, too. Hell, I think the captain would have given me a medal if he could have.

I guess I was lucky, too, that I didn't qualify as a helicopter pilot. If I had, I would have made a career out of the military and probably gotten my butt shot off in Vietnam.

As it was, we had two children with a third on the way when my four-year hitch ended in 1959, and I decided not to re-up. Hell, I was still a private. I kept losing promotions because of all the crap I got into.

Kim was born in 1956 in Plains while I was stationed overseas in Okinawa, and Jana was born in 1958 while I was at Camp LeJeune in North Carolina.

Kim was 18 months old before I saw her. Sybil brought Kim to the airport to greet me when I returned to the states, and Kim started crying when I tried to hold her.

You can see I got off to a good start as a father, and really, I didn't improve much until I got sober.

Sybil enjoyed our life in the Marines, but she didn't have much stomach to be a career military wife. I didn't try to change her mind.

* * *

While I was in the Marines, I began to drink a lot for the first time in my life. I enjoyed it, but it landed me in a pile of trouble.

Drinking kept getting me in trouble time and time again for the next 24 years, but I didn't think about stopping. I couldn't see any relation between my drinking and getting into trouble.

Once I got back in the states, I got busted twice in South Carolina. It seems the local police were a lot less tolerant than the military police overseas. I spent three days in jail in Andrews, South Carolina, for drinking and driving and spent a night in the slammer in Columbia for being drunk in public.

Through the years, I wound up in jail a total of five times. The last time Sybil wouldn't come get me in Buena Vista, and I had to stay overnight. I would've been in jail a lot more, but I finally learned that if I drank with cops, they'd see that I stayed out of trouble.

I wasn't exactly a choir boy overseas. I got into a bunch of fights. My favorite was a free-for-all at a club on a Marine base in Japan. These guys were wanting to dance, and a group of us Southern boys kept putting hillbilly records on the phonograph. It looked like a replay of the Civil War. The South lost again. We damned near got killed.

My boozing in the Marines taught me one important lesson about drinking. There's no excuse for having a hangover. All it takes to cure one is a cold beer or two the morning after.

* * *

I thought I could cuss with anybody when I joined the Marines. But I was an amateur. Stuff like damn and hell was just polite parlor talk.

I had been cussing since I was a boy, but I became a real bad mouth in the Marines. Everybody cussed; everybody drank. But I was on the high end of both.

I tried to tone down my cussing a couple of times, but I finally gave up.

I would lapse right back into cussing when I was sitting around talking, or kidding with someone.

I got a lengthy bleep on the Tom Snyder Radio Show in Los Angeles early this year (1988) for calling Ted Kennedy a name. I told Tom I really wasn't cussing; I was just using a direct quote from somebody else.

It was sort of like old times. I remember the time that Snyder, who's about a foot taller than me, got down on his knees in front of me before we went on the air on his television show and pleaded with me not to use the word "shit" on the air.

I told Tom not to worry. You can guess what the first word out of my mouth was once the show started. Tom broke up laughing.

Other people haven't always been so tolerant of my language. My mouth has gotten me into a lot of trouble, but I'm still not apologizing for things I've said, or how I've said them. I said what I was feeling at the time.

* * *

The four-year period after my discharge from the Marines was a struggle for me. I tried college, working for Jimmy at the warehouse, and some odd jobs. But I was restless and miserable most of the time. I drank a lot during that time.

We returned to Plains from Camp LeJeune, North Carolina, in 1959, and I went to work at the warehouse for Jimmy. Jimmy was now firmly in charge of the business, and he wasn't about to give up any control to me. That didn't keep me from pushing, though.

It was a disaster. I just couldn't accept taking orders from Jimmy.

I guess a lot of it was my fault. I wasn't ready to settle down, and I didn't want to be treated like a dumb kid brother. I thought Jimmy was arrogant and wouldn't listen to anything I had to say. I think I may have still felt a lot of resentment about Jimmy taking over the business when Daddy died.

I finally decided to leave. We went to Atlanta, and I enrolled at Emory University.

Jimmy didn't try to change my mind.

* * *

The job at the warehouse wasn't my only problem in Plains.

I was drinking more and more, and Sybil was beginning to give me a lot of grief about it.

After I'd get off work at the warehouse, I'd head out to Joe Bacon's beer joint, shoot some craps and stay out all hours. When I'd get home, Sybil and I would start arguing. She said I was disgusting and that I always reeked of alcohol.

Looking back at it now, I can see I was drinking alcoholically from the time I was in the Marines. But back then I thought I was just having a good time. And here was Sybil giving me hell about it.

I finally agreed to go to an Alcoholics Anonymous meeting to get her off my back, but I wasn't too happy about it.

* * *

A.A. was a lot different in 1961 than it is today. People were a lot more secretive about it.

Alcoholism was about as fashionable as leprosy back then. People would not go public about their alcoholism twenty five years ago. That didn't start for another 10 to 15 years. Anonymity was a big deal.

Also, most of the old-timers in A.A. thought you had to hit rock bottom before you could be helped.

I drove about 50 miles to Albany to my first A.A. meeting. There were closer meetings, but I went to Albany because I didn't want anybody to know I was going to A.A. I was afraid people would think I couldn't hold my liquor.

I kind of liked A.A. in the beginning and quit drinking for about four months. A.A. wasn't what I expected. It wasn't a bunch of serious religious stuff like I thought. Hell, people were having a pretty good time.

But finally I convinced myself I wasn't an alcoholic. I thought I was too young to be an alcoholic. I was no where near my bottom. That would come 18 years later.

I sort of edged back into drinking to prove to Sybil I wasn't really an alcoholic. I told her I could quit anytime I wanted to. Soon, though, I was up to speed again. I would have seven or eight beers when I drank at night and a case or more on the weekends.

It's 27 years later now, and I've been sober nine years, but I still know if I wanted to bad enough, I could convince myself that it is all right for me to drink—that I'm really not an alcoholic. It scares the hell out of me to realize that. But that fear helps keep me from taking that first drink.

* * *

College life didn't turn out to be much better for me.

I found I just couldn't work full-time and do well in my studies. I had bad study habits to begin with.

I probably made a mistake going to Emory. Maybe I should have tried an easier school. But it probably wouldn't have mattered. I had been away from school too long, and I didn't have any discipline.

CHAPTER EIGHT

I finally dropped out of Emory after Marle (our fourth child) was born. I took a job with a paint company in Macon. I thought things would be better there, but they weren't. I didn't like my job at the paint store. I was drinking more. We were just sort of existing.

If anything, I was more miserable in Macon than I had been in Atlanta or Plains.

* * *

Things changed for me overnight in the spring of 1962.

Jimmy had decided to enter state politics and needed someone to help run the warehouse while he was campaigning for a seat in the Georgia State Senate. He and Mama (who owned a share of the business) decided I was the only logical choice. But I still think Jimmy was a little apprehensive about it after what he and I had been through a couple of years earlier.

Jimmy called me in Macon and asked if I would consider coming back to Plains to run the warehouse operations. I knew right away that I wanted to, but I told Jimmy I would think about it and call him the next day. I didn't want to look too eager.

What made it right for me was that Jimmy had asked me to come back. I never could have ever brought myself to ask Jimmy for a job at the warehouse.

* * *

That was the shot in the arm I needed.

I threw myself into my job, and Sybil and I settled into a large old frame house on North Bond Street, where we lived for the next 15 years.

Every time we had a baby, we would add on another room. Mandy was born in 1968, and Earl was born nine years later. Sybil had three miscarriages along the way.

I was the yard boss at the warehouse. I ran the shelling plant, the storage facilities, the fertilizer business and the cotton gin. During peak season, I had about 50 people working for me, including Jimmy and Rosalynn's three boys.

Jimmy was still boss, and Rosalynn managed the business office. But everything worked out all right this time. Maybe I had matured a little, or Jimmy had lightened up a little because of his outside interests. Or maybe it was a little of both.

Jimmy and I had some disagreements from time to time, but nothing major. I basically dealt with the farmers, and Jimmy dealt with the business end.

* * *

The two Carter brothers also got to know each other for the first time.

"I was very impressed with Billy's ability to relate to farmers, his joviality and his intelligence," Jimmy Carter says. "Billy also worked very hard, which surprised me at first.

"I had always taken pride in my work habits. But when I would get to work at sunrise, Billy would have already been there for an hour or two, chatting with the farmers. His job performance was superb. It was important to Billy that he be beyond criticism when it came to his job performance. Maybe it was his competitive nature, or maybe he wanted to prove something. Whatever his motivation was, he was an exceptional worker.

"Billy was still a hothead at times, but I learned to accept that.

"On a number of occasions when Billy and I would have a strong disagreement, he would storm out of the warehouse and 'scratch off' in his truck for a couple of hours to cool off. Then he would come back to work like nothing had ever happened.

"I knew Billy still drank a lot at night and on the weekends, but I can't recall one instance where he drank at work, or ever missed a day of work, or made a bad decision because of his drinking. And I was with him a lot. During harvest, we practically lived at the warehouse."

* * *

I did manage to sabotage one of the efficiency efforts Jimmy was famous for.

He installed a paging system at the warehouse so he could locate employees and customers on the yard. But I would forget to turn the damned thing off, and you could hear me cussing all over the yard.

Finally, Jimmy decided to scrap the system.

* * *

I purchased a one-sixth interest in the warehouse from Jimmy in 1964. Some people thought Jimmy should have given it to me, but I was just glad to get a chance to own part of the warehouse.

Jimmy's not one to give things away. You might say he's a little on the frugal side.

Two years later, Jimmy decided to run for governor, and I took over management of the warehouse on more or less a full-time basis.

From 1966 on, Jimmy was practically an absentee owner. He lost to Lester Maddox in 1966, which probably galled him worse than his loss to Reagan in 1980. But like I said, Jimmy doesn't give up, and he won the governorship in 1970.

I took over running the business full-time in early 1971, when Jimmy and Rosalynn moved into the Governor's Mansion in Atlanta. Sybil replaced Rosalynn as bookkeeper, and for the next six years, the warehouse was really our show although Jimmy was still majority owner.

It was just about the way Daddy had intended it to be.

* * *

While I was running the warehouse, we expanded it quite a bit. We added a seed business. We built a new warehouse. And we put in a modern shelling plant.

I think I proved my worth.

Most people from outside of Southern Georgia tend to think of me and the gas station, but the peanut business was my heart and soul. The service station was my bar.

* * *

Two of the elder statesmen in the Carters' circle of friends and supporters in Southern Georgia believe that Billy's success in managing the family business was indispensable to Jimmy Carter's successful political career.

Charles Harris, the 67 year old patriarch of Southeastern Georgia Democratic politics, says that without Billy's support in the business, it is doubtful that Jimmy would have been able to enter the race for the 1976 Democratic presidential nomination as early as he did.

"Jimmy began running for president almost as soon as his term as governor ended," says Harris from the counter at his nearly century old department store in downtown Ocilla, Georgia.

"Without that early start, it would have been difficult for Jimmy to gain the momentum he did in the primaries. Billy ran the peanut business first class. He and Sybil stayed at the business day and night to make it success

ful. The entire Carter family benefited from Billy and Sybil's efforts and diligence."

* * *

Arthur Cheokas, a 63 year old Americus, Georgia businessman, is a longtime friend of the Carter family and was one of Jimmy's early supporters for governor and then president. He, too, thinks Billy's success at the business enabled Jimmy to focus almost entirely on politics from 1966 on.

"Billy's got this great sense of humor and likes to have fun," Cheokas says, "but he's very, very serious in business, and he's a hard worker. He's a good businessman. You know where you stand with him, and people like that, particularly the farmers. He's one of the most honest people I've ever known. He was damned important in the scheme of things for Jimmy."

* * *

Jimmy Carter readily acknowledges his brother's contribution to his career. The family business provided virtually the sole means of support for Jimmy Carter and his family in 1975-76 as he made his run for the presidency.

Ruth Carter Stapleton, in her book, Brother Billy, *recalled a poignant scene in the family suite at the Americana Hotel in New York on the night Jimmy Carter received the Democratic presidential nomination.*

Jimmy was thanking all of his supporters when suddenly he focused exclusively on Billy, who was standing next to him.

"Billy, I want to thank you. Without you, it couldn't have happened. You stayed home and kept everything going."

* * *

I was happy when Jimmy won the nomination.

There was no way I could have guessed at the time how our lives were going to change. I don't think Jimmy has ever realized how hard things were for us after he was elected.

I remember one of our girls telling me once how tired she was hearing that her uncle was a son of a bitch. Later on, they heard me called the same thing, or worse.

Jimmy was already well known in Georgia before he was elected president, but it didn't have much effect on Plains or on our day-to-day lives.

The only plus that I can think of for me when Jimmy was governor was that a couple of state troopers went easy on me when they stopped me for drinking and driving. They gave me a ride home, instead of a ticket.

But otherwise, things were pretty normal. If we had a tourist in Plains back when Jimmy was governor, it was some Yankee who had gotten lost on his way to the Andersonville Civil War Cemetery.

CHAPTER NINE

The Carter family has been in Georgia since the late 1700s.

Our family came to Georgia from North Carolina in the 1780s and moved down in this area not too many years later. There's an old Carter Family cemetery about 15 miles north of Plains in Schley County.

My uncle Buddy (Daddy's brother) found it about 20 years ago after looking through old county records. He knew it was out there somewhere.

The cemetery was all grown over when Uncle Buddy found it. I remember going out here to help clear it. You really have to watch for snakes in the Georgia woods, and I'll bet there were hundreds of them out there.

There are about a dozen graves in the main cemetery, and some others in the old slave cemetery behind it. They were my great-great grandfather Wiley Carter's slaves. You can always tell the grave of a slave because the marker has only the first name on it.

I've heard that Wiley Carter was a wealthy landowner. He was born in Georgia in 1798 and died in Schley County in 1864.

My great grandfather and grandfather are buried in other cemeteries not too far from Plains. And Mama and Daddy are buried in Plains.

After I found out I had cancer, one of the first things I wanted to do when I got home was to go to the cemetery to see Mama and Daddy's graves. Sybil thought I was being morbid. I wanted to see for myself if there was enough space in the plot for me — and later for Sybil. I didn't know if I would get that chance again.

Before I went back to the hospital, I asked Jimmy if he and Gloria would mind if I was buried at the foot of Daddy's grave. He agreed, and he got Gloria's permission that same day.

It made me feel a lot better. I thought the cemetery would be my next stop after the hospital.

* * *

In 1983, Billy had made another unusual request of his brother and sister.

Following the death of Miss Lillian, Billy asked Jimmy and Gloria for permission to move Miss Lillian's body from the mortuary to the pond house for public viewing.

Billy thought the mortuary was too impersonal for Miss Lillian, who had spent most of her final years in the pond house, which sits on the bank of a small pond amid tall Georgia pines on a tranquil 14-acre site west of Plains.

After Jimmy and Gloria acceded to Billy's wishes, the mortuary reluctantly went along with the plan.

Gloria says, "The people at the mortuary thought Billy was half crazy. They said people just don't do things like that anymore."

Billy kept a solitary vigil over Miss Lillian's body in the rustic two-story house the night before the funeral. Earlier that evening, Billy's eldest daughter Kim had visited the pond house to touch up Miss Lillian's makeup.

"I asked Daddy if he wanted me or someone to stay with him," Kim recalls. "He said, no, he wanted to be alone with Grandmama."

* * *

I never was one to ask for favors from my brothers and sisters. None of us was that way. We never interfered in each other's lives.

We all helped Jimmy during the primaries and the election, but not to the extent some of other presidential families have. I did a little campaigning in Virginia and Wisconsin, and Sybil and the kids did a lot more. They were part of Jimmy's Peanut Brigade.

It was probably a good thing that I didn't do more campaigning. Jimmy might not have won.

It struck a lot of people as odd that I was running around popping off while Jimmy was in office. He never said a word to me about it, and I never said anything about it to him.

I told other people that I wasn't running for a damned thing, so I would say what I wanted when I wanted.

Still, people weren't used to a first brother like me. I understand Johnson kept his brother, Sam Houston, hog-tied. And I guess Nixon tried to keep his brother under wraps.

* * *

We kids never did confide in each other too much, or talk about family problems.

There was never any argument or any words when Gloria and I quit speaking to each other. I just went my way, and she went hers. And, finally, eight years later, we just started talking again.

We don't discuss our feelings with one another. I think we have a lot of family loyalty, but we have never been a particularly close family.

I was probably closer to Ruth than I was to Jimmy or Gloria. I really appreciated Ruth's support when she came to visit me in Washington during the Libyan investigation. I felt like I was being dumped on and nobody gave a damn. But neither Ruth nor I ever talked about Libya itself or how we felt about it. We just talked mostly about other people and things. We kind of laughed and had a good time.

* * *

In 1980, President Carter was privately angry at his younger brother for his involvement with the unpopular Libyan regime of Colonel Muammar Qaddafi and the resulting Senate investigation to determine whether the president had any knowledge of the extent of his brother's activities. However, President Carter rejected advice to condemn his brother publicly.

"You bet I was mad at Billy," Jimmy Carter says. "His Libyan adventure was devastating to me. I had the Iranian hostage situation on my hands, Ted Kennedy was sniping at me, and the polls were absolutely abysmal. The last thing I needed was to spend hours upon hours of my time and my staff's time defending myself in the Libyan mess.

"Still, I refrained from attacking Billy personally. I loved Billy and felt more protective of him than anything else. He was having financial problems; he and Sybil were having marital problems; and he was fighting hard to recover from his alcoholism, which I sincerely felt had influenced much of what he had done in the Libyan affair.

"Billy and I have never sat down and talked about the whole Libyan matter. I've never conveyed to Billy how I felt, and he's never conveyed his thoughts to me. In fact, there are probably some things I don't want to know."

* * *

The four of us came by our independence honestly. Mama was the most independent person you'd ever want to see, and she raised us to be that way.

I don't remember Mama ever interfering in our lives. She wasn't always happy with what we did, but she didn't say anything about it to us.

But it was a two-way street as far as Mama was concerned. She didn't want us interfering with what she did, either. I was the one who had to take her car away from her when she couldn't drive anymore, and she got mad as hell at me. She wouldn't speak to me for several months.

Mama had strong likes and dislikes, just like I do. And she didn't suffer fools gladly.

You always knew where you stood with Mama. If she didn't like you, she would tell you so in no uncertain terms.

* * *

Family friend, Randy Coleman, whom Miss Lillian and the Carters more or less adopted when he moved to Plains as a teenager, says, "Billy's just like Miss Lillian. He's nicer to pure strangers than he is to someone he doesn't like.

"I remember one time when Billy slipped $100 to a complete stranger with a wife and small children who had stopped by the peanut warehouse in off-season looking for work.

"But if someone he didn't like needed a favor, Billy wouldn't do a thing for him."

* * *

One of Mama's biggest feuds in Plains was with Hugh Carter, who won the State Senate seat Jimmy vacated when he ran for governor.

Mama really disliked Hugh at that time. I think it went back to the time when Hugh jumped on Jimmy's bandwagon in some election only after it became apparent Jimmy was going to win. She never forgave him for that.

We helped Mama get a little revenge a few years later. We (Billy and his service station brain trust) ran (Malcolm) Chicken Wishard against Hugh for his State Senate seat. Chicken was a farmer who liked to hang around the station and drink beer.

Randy Coleman, Hogpen Johnson, and I put up $2000 for Chicken's campaign, and Randy drove Chicken over to Americus to file. We did up posters, buttons and radio commercials, which used a jingle that Tom T. and some of his cronies up in Nasvhille produced.

Mama put up $500 of her own money.

I think we overexposed Chicken. After a while he wasn't another fresh face anymore. But, you know, Chicken almost carried Sumter County.

Mama thought the whole thing was hilarious. She told me that

$500 was one of the best investments she ever made. Hugh never ran for office again. Mama and Hugh finally made peace with each other before she died.

Anyway, it's probably a good thing Chicken lost. If he had won, he probably would have turned out to be just another typical Georgia politician.

* * *

Mama set me up with one of my best lines.

She said: I've got a son who thinks he can be president; a daughter (Ruth) who is a faith-healer; another daughter (Gloria) who rides around on motorcycles; and another son who drinks beer all the time. If I had known they would turn out the way they have, I would have remained a virgin."

I told a variation of the same story to the press when Jimmy was running for president, and it got picked up everywhere.

I said: "I've got a mother who joined the Peace Corps at 68; a brother who wants to be president; a sister who is a holy-roller preacher; and another sister who rides around on motorcycles. I'm the only sane one in the family."

This is my last chance to give Mama proper credit.

* * *

Charles Harris, the Ocilla, Georgia, Democratic Party leader, remembers when Lillian Carter first coined the remark about her children.

"My wife, Esther, and I were having dinner with Miss Lillian in a small restaurant in New York during the '76 Democratic Convention when Miss Lillian said that," Harris says. "Miss Lillian had a wonderful sense of humor, just like Billy. Jimmy was about to be nominated for president of the United States, but I believe she was just as proud of her other children and treasured each of them as unique individuals."

* * *

Another old family friend, Jimmy Murray, proprietor of one of Billy's favorite haunts, the Inn of Americus, says that Miss Lillian never told any of her children what to do, but that she worried about them from time to time.

"Miss Lillian used to come over here to the restaurant for dinner quite often, and frequently, we'd talk together. Several different times she confided in me that she was concerned about Billy's drinking and said she wished with all of her heart that Jimmy and Billy were closer.

"I tried to get these messages across to Billy without betraying Miss Lillian's confidence, but never had much luck. I know Miss Lillian would be happy today about the fact that Billy's still not drinking and that he and Jimmy have grown much closer."

* * *

Mama was a nurse when she was younger and had always wanted to work with the poor. So she just up and joined the Peace Corps in 1966 at the age of 68 and spent two years working with the poor in India.

That experience really affected Mama. If anything, I think it made her less tolerant of frivolous things and frivolous people.

Mama and I were real close for the last 20 years of her life.

I saw a lot of strength in Mama that I didn't see while Daddy was alive. She joined the Peace Corps; she overcame one illness after another; and she had the will to do what she wanted no matter what anyone said or thought. She thought Jimmy and I would try to talk her out of joining the Peace Corps. But both Jimmy and I knew there was no sense in trying to get Mama to change her mind.

Like I said earlier, I can't believe Mama had the gumption to thumb her nose at convention in a small town like Plains. People normally just don't do that. But Mama didn't give a damn about what people thought.

* * *

I was amazed, too, at how Mama handled dying.

After Ruth died (in the summer of 1983), it was like Mama decided that it was time for her to go. Simple as that. Before she went to the nursing home for the final time, Mama asked each grandchild to come by to visit her, one-by-one. After she had seen the last grandchild, she said: "I don't want to see them again, or for them to see me again before I die." That was the last time she saw the grandkids or asked about them.

Mama and I had a lot in common.

We liked and disliked most of the same people, and liked a lot of the same things. I don't believe I was Mama's favorite, like a lot of people think, because I don't think Mama had favorites. She said at times that I needed her love and attention more than the others did, which was probably true, but that didn't make me her favorite.

As much as anything, Mama and I both liked a good argument.

I'm a big sports fan, baseball in particular, and I liked to tease

Mama about her passion for sports. She especially liked wrestling, of all things.

Mama had the first satellite dish in Plains so she could watch baseball and wrestling at all hours. She also would get Randy Coleman to drive her to the wrestling matches in Columbus. I wouldn't take her because she would go crazy at the matches. I remember one time she came home raving about how her favorite wrestler had broken his leg.

I told her: "Hell, Mama, he's faking. I'll bet you $50 he's back in the ring tomorrow night."

She got mad at me and called me on the bet. Sure enough, her wrestler was back the very next night. Mama sent me the $50 in the mail, and didn't speak to me again for three months.

That's how all of our arguments ended. She just quit talking to me.

* * *

I still miss Mama. But she was 84 when she died in 1983, and I was prepared for her death.

Mama had lived a long, full life, and she was ready to go. I wasn't prepared for Ruth's death. It all happened so quick.

* * *

Ruth died in the summer of 1983 at 52 in Fayetteville, North Carolina. Ruth had spent New Year's with us, and during her whole visit, she was bothered by severe back pain. We had no idea what her problem was, but cancer never entered my mind. Within a matter of days or weeks, we found out she had pancreatic cancer.

It was tough for her, and for all of us.

Ruth chose not to have conventional treatment. She believed in healing through prayer.

I didn't agree with that, but Ruth believed strongly in what she was doing. She never once tried to force her religion on any of us, and I sure as hell wasn't going to try to convince her she was wrong.

Sybil and I visited Ruth in the hospital in North Carolina a few days before she died.

Her spirits were fine, but she had just wasted away. I sometimes wish we hadn't seen her that way. Ruth had always been so full of life.

I've thought about that a lot since I found out I had cancer.

CHAPTER TEN

Sybil

I've always said life with Billy wasn't easy, but it was never boring.

From the time I first met him when I was in the third grade, he was always in the center of a storm.

A lot of people might think Billy's behavior changed when Jimmy was elected president. But he didn't change one iota. The only difference was that he received more attention.

There wasn't a phony bone in Billy's body. He was a good ol' boy and redneck through and through, and proud of it.

It makes me mad that the term redneck has taken on such a negative connotation. Rednecks are really just Southern farmers whose necks are red from bending over and working in the fields under the hot sun.

Billy wasn't a redneck in that sense because he never worked in the fields. But he was a redneck at heart. He dealt with South Georgia farmers like he was one of them. He trusted them, and they trusted him. That's the way he ran the peanut business.

We were happy as a family when Billy was running the warehouse. But until Billy got sober, Billy, without the warehouse, was like a duck out of water. At times, he was nearly impossible to live with.

* * *

Billy's two big crises in our first twenty-five years together both revolved around the warehouse. First, he found that he couldn't work for Jimmy after the Marines, and later, he lost control of the warehouse after Jimmy was elected president.

Both times his drinking picked up considerably. And our family life went to pieces.

When Billy was drinking, he found fault with everything. Nothing would please him. He criticized me, the children, and everything we did. The children would just walk around on tiptoes when he had been drinking, and I wouldn't say anything for fear of starting an argument.

I had been raised Southern, and I didn't know how to talk about problems or feelings. There were times when I wished things were different, but I never said anything about those wishes to Billy or anyone.

That would all change when I received treatment, but in the 60s and early 70s, I put all my energies into being a good mother, making excuses for Billy's drinking, and keeping peace at home.

What puzzled me at the time was that I knew Billy was a generous, caring, loving, sweet person, but I wasn't seeing that in him at home, particularly in the last two or three years before he quit drinking.

I became jealous of Billy's relationship with his friends. He was always teasing, joking and giving to his friends, but he could be a totally different person with us. Billy was never abusive physically, but he was verbally abusive to me and the children.

It was the alcohol, of course, but I didn't realize that. I kept thinking if I could do this or that differently, he wouldn't drink so much, and things would be better.

And when he apparently cut back some on his drinking during those years at the warehouse, I thought everything was going to be okay.

* * *

It was anything but love at first sight for Billy and me. When I first met Billy after moving to Plains from Alabama, I didn't like him.

He seemed to be a lot different than the other boys. He appeared to be kind of hard-bitten and uncaring, like he had a chip on his shoulder.

I tried to stay out of his way at first, but once I got to know him I found out he was really a little bit shy and self-conscious. I also began to see this "little boy" in him, which never really went away even after he was grown.

Our friend Buck Sappenfield always teased me about having seven children instead of six and said I did a poor job of raising the oldest one, which, of course, was Billy.

Billy and I were opposites in many ways.

Billy was always carefree and kind of reckless, and I was serious and stable.

Even though I was two years younger, I was much more mature than Billy when we were young. I felt like I had been grown half my life when Billy and I decided to get married. My mother worked, so I shared in the washing, the house cleaning and the cooking.

I felt kind of hemmed in at home so I was ready to get married at 16, when Billy proposed. I didn't think about waiting to get married. I knew I loved Billy and wanted to be his wife.

* * *

Even before we got married, I knew there would be some stormy seas ahead.

Billy was always extremely jealous and possessive. In fact, the whole Carter family is possessive—not in material things, but in relationships. Jimmy is certainly that way with Rosalynn, and I think Miss Lillian was that way with all of her kids.

They learned to accept me as part of the family, but in the early part of our marriage, I always had the feeling that the Carters thought I wasn't quite bright enough and well-read enough to take an equal part in their discussions.

Billy's possessiveness showed up in a lot of ways. Once he became so angry when I refused to ride with him to a ball game that he rammed his fist through a window at school. Another time, he started a fight at a square dance when I danced with someone else.

Billy had a real bad temper, and it became even worse after Mister Earl died. He began to be openly rebellious. He was bitter that Miss Lillian didn't hold the business for him until he was ready to run it, and he didn't like the way Jimmy treated him. Those were bad times for him, but I was always able to see the loving, sweet caring person in him. The problem was he was lost and hurt, and he didn't know how to express it.

I feel like Jimmy should have given Billy more consideration. If anything, Jimmy was always indulging Billy, which didn't help Billy develop any self-confidence. Billy felt like Jimmy didn't think he had what it took to be successful.

Years later, I noticed that Billy seemed to use Jimmy as a model on how to discipline the children. Mister Earl had spanked Billy only twice in his life, and Billy didn't know diddly about discipline. Jimmy's three boys, Chip, Jack and Jeff, all worked at the warehouse, and Billy would observe how Jimmy treated them and try to emulate him in disciplining our son, Buddy. It didn't work because it wasn't natural to Billy, and he ended up being too hard on

Buddy. Billy came to realize that later, but only after a lot of friction developed between him and Buddy.

Billy was possessive of me in other ways, too.

He was jealous of the time I spent with my family. Sometimes he would get angry when I stayed over at my family's house too long or if my father and I went fishing by ourselves. When he was angry, he would refuse to go to my parents' house for dinner and wouldn't offer any excuses. He always left it up to me to make excuses.

We rarely went out with couples. He and I would go out together by ourselves, or he would go out drinking with the boys. Like a fool, I never complained.

I can see now his behavior was alcoholic behavior, even though he didn't appear to be drinking all that heavily at the time. And I permitted that behavior to continue by making excuses for him and always being at his beck and call.

Billy used to joke that women should be kept barefoot and pregnant. The trouble was for many, many years I'm not sure he was joking. But once I stopped enabling him, he changed. And he meant it.

* * *

One thing Billy and I agreed on from the start is that we wanted a big family.

We didn't waste any time. Kim and Jana were born while Billy was in the Marines. Each time, though, I came back to Plains to have the baby. Billy hated military hospitals, and didn't want me to go near them.

We called Billy in Okinawa to tell him about Kim, and I remember him asking, "Are all the holes in the right place?"

Buddy was born after we came back to Plains the first time; Marle was born while Billy was a student at Emory; Mandy was born in Plains; and Little Earl was born in Plains shortly before Jimmy was elected president.

Billy was never more attentive to me than when I was pregnant. And when I had a miscarriage between Buddy and Marle, and again between Marle and Mandy, and Mandy and Earl, he was gentle, sweet and caring.

Billy had a great way around changing diapers. He would lay the kids on a clean sheet with no diaper on, and then change the sheet when it got soiled. He always said he was afraid he'd stick them with a pin if he tried to change their diapers.

We didn't have much money then, but we were rich in sheets. We must have had 50 of them.

I should have savored Billy taking care of things, but I didn't. I felt vaguely guilty about the miscarriages. I felt like they were my fault; that I had done something wrong. I was already a perfect co-dependent.

* * *

We had a good life while Billy was in the Marines, even though we had some hard times. While Billy was in basic training, I got pregnant and caught the measles, and we were nearly broke most of the time.

One time, we were down to our last quarter and had to choose between buying a loaf of bread and bus fare for me to go to work. Billy insisted I use it for bus fare because I was pregnant and he thought it wouldn't be good for me to walk to work.

I don't think anything bothered us too much then because we were on our own for the first time, and it was an adventure for us.

After the Marines, things went down hill for us for a while. I had hoped Billy would settle into work at the warehouse, but I understood his reason for leaving. He and Jimmy just weren't hitting it off. Jimmy treated him too much like a kid brother.

College didn't work out for Billy, either, but we really hit bottom at Macon, where Billy worked at the paint store. Billy hated his job and began drinking heavily again. He had been drinking all along except for that period when he was in A.A., but it became worse in Macon.

He flirted with A.A. again, but this time, he didn't take it as seriously as the first time. I was really beginning to despair for us and felt powerless to do anything about it.

I was almost at my wit's end when Jimmy called to ask Billy to return to the warehouse to work. Billy says he mulled it over for a night, but I don't remember anything of the sort. He jumped at the chance. We were practically packed within an hour after Billy talked to Jimmy.

* * *

I really thought our struggles were behind us when we returned to Plains.

Working at the warehouse together were some the happiest times of our lives. I felt like we finally had something that belonged to us. Buddy and the girls worked at the warehouse, and I became the full time bookkeeper when Jimmy was elected governor.

We'd work around the clock from mid-August to mid-September during peanut harvest, but I enjoyed every minute of it. We were working together as a family.

Things were going so well on the surface that, like a fool, I ignored the problems under the surface. Billy didn't drink at work and was a good provider for us, but he spent all of his spare time out drinking with the boys. He was never home and never did family things.

I would fuss at him from time to time about his drinking, but he would just storm out of the house and disappear when I did. And he continued to get into fights when he was out drinking.

I asked Jimmy to talk to Billy about his drinking a couple of times, but both times, Billy just shined Jimmy on. We were all so ignorant about alcoholism and how to deal with it.

What made it difficult for us was that Billy was so likeable and generous most of the time, and we wanted to believe him when he promised he would watch his drinking.

Billy could always make a joke of his behavior. Once he received a letter of censure from the Moose Club in Americus after getting into a fight there in which he lost a front tooth. The letter said Billy's conduct was "ungentlemanly."

Billy wrote back that if he had been a true gentleman to begin with, he never would have joined the Moose Club.

Billy was always like that. One minute you would want to kill him, and the next minute you'd forget why you were so mad at him.

CHAPTER ELEVEN

Sybil

The kids' life with Billy wasn't always easy, either, particularly for the four older children.

But, thank God, Billy had a chance to make amends to them all and to be an attentive father to Earl and Mandy for the last nine years of his life.

Billy always loved his children and would do anything for them, but his alcoholism had a real effect on Kim, Jana, Buddy and Marle when they were growing up. He said time and time again that his greatest regret about his drinking was the pain it caused the children. He also regretted missing those years with the kids.

All the kids responded really well to Billy's cancer, including Little Earl. They accepted it. Marle told me that she knew her father wasn't going to be with us as long as she would like, but she just wasn't going to think about his dying as long as he was alive.

Mandy, who was only 19 at the time, said when she first saw Billy in the Intensive Care Unit at Emory after he came out of surgery, she decided then and there Billy wasn't going to get any better unless we all helped him. Up until that point, Mandy was just miserable. She said the day her father underwent surgery at Emory was "the longest day of her life."

The children's attitude helped Billy; and his helped them. Everyone kept things as positive and as normal as possible, right to the very end.

Billy told me in the hospital what he wanted more than anything else was for the kids to go about their day-to-day lives as if nothing had happened.

Billy had his low moments after that, though, and when he thought that his condition wasn't going to improve, he asked Mandy to promise him that she would finish college before she got married. That's the only time I remember Billy giving into the thought of dying around the children.

Most of the time, he made these awful grisly jokes about dying, and the kids would just shrug him off. That's the way he wanted them to react. Billy was not the sentimental type.

* * *

Billy really was two different fathers. He was sometimes a distant, very strict father with the four older children, and a real giving father to the two youngest, Mandy and Earl.

Shortly after he got sober, he tried to make up for all those hard years with Kim, Jana, Buddy and Marle. But he finally realized he couldn't change the past and began concentrating on the present.

The older children were amazed at how lenient Billy was with Mandy and Earl.

Marle told me that the first time she heard Mandy talk back to Billy she almost fainted. Billy didn't tolerate back-talk from the four older kids, even when he knew they were right.

At first I think the older kids resented how Billy treated Mandy and Earl, but I believe they are over that now. They realize that Billy's drinking had a lot to do with how he was with them. All of them are working through that one way or another.

Buddy probably understands alcoholism better than the others since he participated in the Long Beach family program for about a week while his father and I were there. But understanding alcoholism and coming to grips with how it affected you personally are two different things. I know that from experience, and I think Buddy does, too.

* * *

Anyone who knows much about alcoholism knows about the effects it can have on the children.

I've encouraged the kids to go to self-help meetings and talk about their feelings. Billy wanted that, too, but he left the persuading up to me, as usual. Some things never change, no matter how long someone's been sober.

Too, I think Billy never really got through all of his guilt with the older children and had a lot of trouble talking to them about how his drinking might have affected them.

Kim and Buddy were probably more aware of Billy's drinking and its impact on them than either Jana or Marle.

Jana still has a lot of denial about her Daddy's drinking, but I think Marle is gradually beginning to realize how it affected her. Marle went out of her way to keep things running smoothly at home when her daddy had been drinking, and I'm sure it took a toll on her, just like it did on me.

CHAPTER ELEVEN

Marle was still living at home when Billy's drinking was at its worst. And she thought if she did everything perfectly, things would be peaceful at home when Billy was there.

With their Daddy's drinking and touring all around the country and their uncle being president, it's a wonder the kids did as well as they did. They rarely caused us a moment's concern.

They are wholesome, kind of All-American-looking kids. I always told Billy they got their good looks from my side of the family.

Everyone credits me with raising such good kids, but the credit should go to them. I was so busy rushing around trying to see that their needs and Billy's needs were being met, it's a wonder I did anything right.

I think I've been a much better mother to all of them since I found my independence through treatment.

* * *

I'll let the kids tell their own stories of life with their father. Kim and Jana both felt a little nervous about talking about their feelings because they didn't want to sound negative. But Billy and I both encouraged them to tell it like it was.

* * *

Kim Carter Fuller, 31, is a teacher of English Literature and Grammar at Tri-County High School, north of Plains. She and her husband, Mark, have a daughter, Amanda (Little Mandy), age 5, and a son, Wayne Robert, who was born December 28, 1988.

I was never close to Daddy while I was growing up. I always felt like I had to do really well for Daddy to pay any attention. I felt much closer to him once I was grown, but it was still hard for me to talk with him one-on-one.

Daddy was very strict with us when we were young. I remember asking him if I could get my ears pierced when I was about 16. He told me "no," and then just sat there and laughed when I started crying. I think he was drunk at the time.

It seems like I cried all the time. I was grounded a lot and didn't have my first real date until I was 17.

When he was drinking, Daddy would holler an awful lot and criticize everything we did. When he and Mama would argue, Daddy would just leave the house and not come back. Things got to the point where we were glad when Daddy was gone. Everything was so peaceful then.

I would get angry a lot, but I was never angry enough to risk talking back to Daddy. He was always going to get the last word in.

I knew Daddy liked to have fun, but we were never a real part of it except at the gas station. We had a lot of fun at the station, but Mama really didn't like us hanging around there.

Mark traveled with Daddy when he was touring around the country after Uncle Jimmy was elected president, and even though Mark and I weren't married yet, we got caught in some awkward spots between Mama and Daddy. Mark would tell me that Mama would quiz him about Daddy's behavior and ask him not to let Daddy do this or that.

Once, Mama and I went to Nashville where Daddy was appearing on a show, and Mark said it drove him crazy looking after Mama and me, as well as Daddy. He was always trying to keep Daddy out of trouble.

Daddy didn't participate in many family things when we were growing up. The only things I remember him doing with us were around Christmas time. Once it snowed, and he pulled us around on a sled, and another time, I remember him teaching Buddy and Jana Kae how to ride their new bikes.

We mostly looked to Mama for support. I was also close to my Granddaddy Spires (Sybil's father) and to Grandmama (Miss Lillian).

I knew Daddy drank too much, but the first time he ever embarrassed me with his drinking was at a high school basketball game in Albany. I was there with a group of my friends, and Daddy was there with some of his drinking buddies. When Daddy got up to leave, he was so drunk that he fell down some steps. I know my friends noticed, but they never said a word to me. I was so embarrassed I could have died.

Another time in college, a professor who didn't know who I was went into a long dissertation about Daddy in class. He said the reason Daddy was so bloated was because he was malnourished due to his drinking. I felt like crawling under my chair.

Daddy mellowed a lot after he quit drinking, but it took him a couple of years to really change.

Mark and I got married not long after Daddy came back from

treatment, and he got angry at me for dropping a glass at a bridal shower. He told me he wasn't going to give away such a clumsy daughter. He called me a couple of days later and apologized. It was one of the few times I ever heard him apologize to someone. I knew then that he had changed.

Mama had changed, too. Daddy got mad at her at home once, and Mama just laughed at him. It almost floored us.

Daddy was always a good daddy to us despite his drinking.

You never could stay mad at Daddy for long. He would do something really funny, or kind.

I remember him coming home once with blood all over a brand new jacket that he really loved. He had stopped to help out at a real bad traffic accident and had wrapped a little baby who was in the wreck in his jacket and held the baby up close to him to keep him warm.

Daddy was like that. If you ever needed help, you always knew you could count on him.

I was real proud of Daddy early on when Uncle Jimmy was president. He was funny on the talk shows and in the interviews he did. But the Libyan thing bothered me. I just couldn't understand why he got involved with the Libyans. I didn't know that he was having financial problems at the time.

Daddy was always extremely generous to us kids. He helped Mark and me get financing for our home in Plains. He would give you the shirt off his back if you needed it.

I came to realize he was a very feeling person. I remember seeing him cry for the first time at Aunt Ruth's funeral in 1983 and how tender he was when Grandmama died.

None of us will ever forget how he handled his cancer. I think that will be my lasting memory of him.

* * *

Jana Kae Carter, 29, lives in Plains and is a bookkeeper for a nursing home in nearby Americus, Georgia. She has a son, Billy, age eight, from a marriage which ended in divorce.

Mama, Kim, Aunt Ruth — everyone—says I'm more like Daddy than the other kids. That's probably true. I do what I want, and don't care what other people think, just like Daddy did.

I admired Daddy for not taking any bull off anyone. I also admired him for his intelligence and for the way he helped other people. He'd always be the first person to help someone get a loan, or get someone out of jail.

He would do anything in the world for us kids, too; but he never knew how to say, "I love you."

I was scared of Daddy when I was living at home. I would say anything to anybody away from home, but there was no way I would voice a contrary opinion to Daddy. I would just walk around him on tiptoes.

People were always telling me Daddy drank too much, but I didn't know he had a drinking problem. I would just see him drinking beer and having a lot of fun. It surprised me when he went into treatment for alcoholism, but when he got back, I could tell he was different.

Daddy always kept an eye on me—maybe because I was like him. I don't think either he or Mama ever really trusted me.

At times, I felt like the black sheep of the family. I was always in one kind of trouble or another, and I felt big, fat and ugly around the others. I couldn't sing; I couldn't dance; and I was the only one who seemed to have bad luck—like with my marriage, my cancer, my jobs, you name it.

A few years ago, I accidentally set fire to my house, and the damn thing burned to the ground. I wasn't concerned about the house or my possessions; I was afraid Daddy was going to kill me when he found out.

Instead, he came rushing over and asked me if Little Billy and I were all right. He told me not to worry about the house and my things; he'd take care of that. I just stood there speechless.

There were plenty of times when I know Daddy felt like killing me, like the time Buddy and I ran away from home when we were kids, or when Daddy found out I had been chasing Buddy around with a knife.

He would also get mad at me about things like sitting in his favorite chair or not shaving my legs. Kim, Marle and I couldn't even wear make-up without his approval. We'd appeal to Mama, but she didn't have much luck with him either.

Daddy, though, never got on me for saying what I thought to people—even to Grandmama (Miss Lillian). Grandmama and I fought like cats and dogs. When Uncle Jimmy was president, Buddy and I would throw rocks at the tourists, and one time, Buddy "mooned" the back car of the tourist train. I also called some man a bastard at the train station gift shop where I worked when the guy said something bad about Daddy.

Daddy never reprimanded me about any of that stuff.

I cried every day for a week or so when we found out Daddy had inoperable cancer. I got my mourning out of the way and tried not to think about it anymore.

I've also accepted that I had cancer, but I really don't worry about it returning. I worried much more about Daddy's cancer.

* * *

William Alton (Buddy) Carter, 27, lives in Franklin, Tennessee, near Nashville, where he is in the landscaping business. He and his wife, Marlene, have a four year old son, Will.

I loved my father, but I was never as close to him as I was my mother.

The only time I ever really felt comfortable talking to Daddy is when we were talking business. I didn't feel comfortable talking about other things with him, and I don't think he did, either.

When he was sick, he told me things he wanted me to do when he was gone, like looking after Mother. But we never went deeper than that.

At times, I wish things could have been different between us, but it wasn't meant to be.

In Daddy's mind, he had figured out what I was supposed to do from the day I was born. And when I didn't do it the way he wanted, he was angry. When I told him I was quitting the mobile home business, where I was working with him, and moving to Nashville, he blew his stack. I told him I had a job offer in Nashville, which wasn't true, to try to keep a little peace.

I worked with my father at the warehouse from the time I was six, up until he left the business when I was 16 or 17. He was a good businessman, but he was a hard man to work for. He had me doing things a kid my age shouldn't have had to do. When we put in the peanut sheller at the warehouse, he made me learn every little detail about it, even though I was only 11 or 12 at the time.

Later, when I worked with him in the mobile home business, I remember him telling me that if I didn't make somebody cry when I fired them or chewed them out, then I wasn't being tough enough. I decided if that's what it took to be a good businessman, I didn't want to be one.

Daddy was happiest when he was at the warehouse. He loved

dealing with farmers and getting up at 4:30 in the morning to go out and talk with them.

The gas station was a lot of fun for me. I hung out there all I could and was sort of like a pet or mascot. The gas station was a great education for me, listening to all the old-timers and shooting craps and playing cards with them.

I didn't notice a lot of difference in Daddy when he quit drinking. My mother was the one who really changed. To me, he was still the same Billy Carter without the drinking.

I spent a week in Long Beach in the family program, and at first, I really resented it. I thought my father's the problem, not me. Now, I've come to realize that alcoholism is a family problem, but it took a while.

When Daddy got home from treatment, it was like he thought, okay, the drinking is behind me, now we can become a real father and son. I didn't feel that way. I couldn't forget the first 18 years of my life that fast.

I remember when I was a kid I would look out the window when Daddy got home to see what kind of mood he was in. If he was in a bad mood, I just disappeared. When he was in a good mood, it was great. He would sit around telling these funny stories. He was a great storyteller.

I was on the road with my father when his drinking became real bad. He didn't even try to hide it from me. On some mornings, I saw him drink a full pint before he even got out of bed. I also remember him clinking when he walked because of the airline miniatures he had stuffed in his pocket. Neither he nor I ever said a word about his drinking.

My father was tough on me, but I always knew he would do anything in the world for us kids if we needed help.

I really admired how Daddy handled his illness. I don't think anybody could have dealt with it any better than he did. He was cracking jokes to the very end, which helped put us at ease around him.

I think the thing that bothered him most when he was ill was that he couldn't be as active as he wanted. I don't think the physical pain bothered him nearly half as much. He had a very active mind and was one of the most intelligent people I've ever known.

He was probably the best "Trivial Pursuit" player in the world. If he ever missed an answer, which was rare, he would insist the answer on the game card was wrong. And sometimes he was right.

* * *

Marle Carter Usry, 25, has taken a leave of absence from her teaching job at Rama Road Elementary School in Charlotte, North Carolina, to be with her son, William Luke, who was born in September 1988. Marle's husband, Jody, is a salesman with Hormel Company in Charlotte.

Daddy was like a god to me. I don't ever remember him disciplining me, but I don't think I ever gave him reason to.

For some reason, I always knew Daddy was very vulnerable, and I felt very protective of him. Still, I knew Daddy had a bad temper and that things could become very traumatic at home when he was in a bad mood. I'm sure his drinking was at the root of the problem, but I didn't think about it at the time. I just tried to do things right around home to keep everything running smoothly.

I made sure Daddy's steak was done just right, that we had cloth napkins on the table, because Daddy hated paper napkins, and that we had plenty of ice and so forth. Once, I remember Daddy went into a rage when he discovered that we were out of ice and gave me $50 to go out and buy all the ice trays in Plains.

Even though I'm a middle child, I felt like the oldest during the period when Uncle Jimmy was president. I stayed home a lot, out of the spotlight, and cooked and kept house. I also assumed responsibility for shielding Mandy and Earl from all the crowds. I built up a wall around me and wouldn't let anybody in except for family members.

I think Daddy felt guilty because he was gone a lot and he compensated for it by showering us with money or gifts. Once, right out of the blue, he bought us a pinball machine, and other times he would give me $50 or $100 for some small favor like cleaning out his sock drawer.

I knew Daddy drank a lot, but I was surprised when I heard on the radio for the first time that he was an alcoholic. I was concerned about what my friends would think. I had always made excuses for Daddy or taken up for him when my friends asked me about something he had done. But I didn't know what to say when I heard he was an alcoholic. Mama talked to us about Daddy's drinking, and that helped a lot. She made sure we kids didn't miss out on anything.

My first inkling that Daddy was having problems came late one night after a party at our house. He came into my room and said, "Marle, I hope that you are never ashamed of me." He tried to conceal his tears, but I could tell he was crying. I told Daddy that I loved him and was never ashamed of anything he did, but inwardly, I was scared for him. I knew then he was in real trouble.

It was a crazy period for us when Uncle Jimmy was president. We received threats all the time. Once I remember answering the phone and some man said there was a bomb at the filling station and that it was going to go off in a few minutes at 6 o'clock.

Other people would call and say what they were going to do to us, or Daddy. It was frightening.

But there were plenty of good times, too. I met a lot of famous people like Begin and Sadat, Senator John Glenn, John Denver, Anson Williams of "Happy Days," and so on. That's what I look back on now, plus the good times we had with Daddy after he quit drinking.

The hurts always go away.

* * *

Mandy Carter, 21, is a junior at Georgia Southwestern University in Americus, Georgia, and is a reporter for Americus' daily newspaper. She lives at home in Plains.

I was pretty young when Daddy was at the height of his celebrity, and I really don't remember a lot of things. I felt more like Daddy was a movie star. I thought, wow, he's always on the Donahue show, or some television show, and people recognize him everywhere we go. It was really pretty exciting for an 8 or 10-year-old like me.

I remember the Libyan affair pretty well. It broke in the summertime, and Mama warned us: "Your Daddy's going to be on the news a lot, and I don't want you to believe anything you hear without checking it with me."

The only real difficulty for me when Uncle Jimmy was in office was in the way my friends related to me. Some of my classmates just assumed I would be stuck up, or too big for my britches, and shied away from me. Most of my friends, though, were always telling me that they liked my daddy better than my uncle.

I don't remember Daddy being drunk when I was young and really didn't understand when he went away for treatment in California. When he got back from California, I wanted to ask him what they did to him out there, but I was afraid to. One thing I noticed was that he sure looked different. He had lost weight and had a mustache and a tan.

I know my older sisters and Buddy were always envious of how lenient Daddy was with Earl and me. But I thought he was fairly strict with me. I wasn't afraid to argue with either Mama or Daddy. I would sit and butt heads with Daddy, but, finally, he would give me this stern look over his glasses, and I'd know the argument was over.

Sometimes I think he tried too hard to be firm with us. He would nearly choke when I wore a strapless dress, but I would just ignore his comments until he stopped. He was concerned about us and didn't want to let go, but usually he did.

He told me once no matter what decision or mistake I made, he'd always stand behind me. I think all of us kids knew that.

To me, Daddy was always one of the funniest people I had ever known. Nobody ever knew what to expect from him. He was an original.

When Daddy was in the hospital in Atlanta, he got out of his wheelchair to get off the elevator and a nurse told him, "Mr. Carter, you can't get out of your wheelchair."

Daddy said, "Like hell I can't," and just walked off.

There were a lot of sad moments in the last year of Daddy's life, but for the most part, we were really happy and very close as a family.

After he had come home from the hospital for the first time, I walked into Daddy's room and found him crying. I think he was a little embarrassed. He told me not to worry. He said he wasn't going to be sad all the time, and he wasn't going to give up.

* * *

Earl Carter is 12 years old and an avid sports fan and collector of baseball cards. He is a sixth grader and a second baseman on the Webster County Little League baseball team.

Daddy always teased me a lot, more than other dads teased their kids. But I learned to give it right back to him. I think he liked that. It was fun.

One time Daddy said I looked like a zombie when I let a ball go by me at second base, and I told him, "You don't look so swift yourself." He thought that was funny.

Daddy loved to tease us. He would tease Mandy about her cooking. One time, he told Mandy that her pork chops looked like rocks and tasted even worse.

Mostly, he teased me about baseball and girls. He got on me about not eating and about my schoolwork. When I wouldn't eat, Daddy would shout out to Mama in the kitchen, "Sybil, Earl doesn't like your cooking." I would make a face at him.

I was worried about Daddy when he got sick. Uncle Jimmy was the one who told me Daddy had cancer. Uncle Jimmy got me out of school and said I needed to know because he was sure that the news about Daddy was going to be on television.

When I saw Daddy, he told me not to worry and said everything was going to be fine for me. I was happy when he started feeling better, and we got to do things together.

Daddy and I have done a lot together since he got out of the hospital. We went to a Braves game in Atlanta and the Atlanta 500 car race. I met a lot of people who knew Daddy, and it was fun. I also went fishing with Uncle Jimmy and Daddy, and that was a lot of fun, too.

I liked it when Daddy would help me with baseball and when we would feed the fish at the pond by Uncle Jimmy's house. I know Daddy didn't feel too well sometimes, but because he wasn't working we got to spend more time together than ever before.

Daddy and I always had fun together.

CHAPTER TWELVE

Billy

I was down to at the old gas station this spring and began reminiscing with a friend about what things were like in Plains a dozen years ago when Jimmy was elected president.

As we talked, I was looking out toward the depot from the gas station at the little downtown park, which isn't half as big as a football field, and the few old red brick buildings beyond it. I wondered out loud: "How in the hell did we manage to pack 20,000 tourists a day into Plains?"

Things just don't seem real anymore about that period. They didn't seem too real when they were happening.

I sold the gas station in 1981, a step ahead of the IRS, which had red tagged it and everything else I owned. A few others have owned the station since. Most of them tried to capitalize on the tourist trade, but when that faded away, they did, too.

A local guy, Bobby Salter, owns the station now. He's concentrating on getting local business, and doing a good job. Everything's full service at Bobby's station. When you pull in, they wash your windshield, check the air in your tires—just like the old days. And around lunch time you can get some good barbecue that they cook up on an old grill off the side of the station.

Except for some fresh paint, the station looks about the same from the outside as it did when I had it. But there's one big difference. Bobby doesn't sell beer.

Hell, I never would have bought the station in the first place if I couldn't have sold beer.

The station was my bar and my club. It was the only high-end drinking establishment in Plains for about nine years.

* * *

I bought the station back in 1972 when I sensed there was a chance for Plains to go "wet." To make sure it happened, I got myself elected to the City Council to help swing the vote on the sale of beer in the city limits.

Up until then, the only beer joint around was Joe Bacon's on the outskirts of town, where I did most of my serious drinking and crap shooting. They later changed the name of Joe's place to the

Plains Country Club. People from out of town would see or hear the name "Plains Country Club" and think that we had a fancy golf course in town.

People around town knew the only reason I wanted to be on the council was to vote in beer sales, and a lot of them were up in arms about it. Some of the Baptists thought I was the reincarnation of the devil.

The whole issue was a slam dunk once I got on the council. The final vote on beer sales was 3 to 2, and I began selling beer at the station. I resigned from the council right after that.

Really, the whole thing turned out to be a good deal for Plains. To win the vote, I agreed to a five-cent city tax on each can of beer sold, and the beer tax became the biggest source of revenue for the town.

The town made more money off my beer sales than I did. I had to pay the tax on all beer coming into the station, and as anybody can tell you, I probably drank or gave away more beer than I sold.

* * *

I couldn't believe how the press and the tourists took to the gas station after Jimmy was elected president.

I sure didn't do anything special to attract them, other than maybe run off my mouth. Somebody suggested that we spruce the place up after Jimmy was in office, like most businesses around town were doing, but I said I would shoot anybody who so much as laid a paintbrush on the place.

My cousin Hugh called the station an "eyesore" in his book *Cousin Beedie and Cousin Hot*, but I said, hell, it was an eyesore before Jimmy was elected, and I sure wasn't going to change it just because he was president.

The first four years I had the station, it was mostly a hangout for my friends and the men around town, like Mr. Jack Pugh, who was in his 70s. Hogpen Johnson, Bud Duvall, Chicken Wishard, Doug Unger, Randy Coleman and about dozen other regulars would sit around and shoot the breeze and drink beer. We'd also shoot craps up against one of the drink boxes. I won a lot of money shooting craps against that old drink box.

I'd head over to the station right after work at the warehouse. I think Sybil preferred me hanging out there rather than at Joe Bacon's or some other place. At least, she usually knew where I was.

CHAPTER TWELVE

It was a major imposition for us when someone wanted to buy some gas. We were a beer joint that sold gas as a sideline.

* * *

After Jimmy was elected, we tried to keep things as normal as possible at the station. But the whole town had become a sideshow, and the station was in the center ring.

During the height of things, we were selling 2000 cases of beer a week and pumping 40,000 to 50,000 gallons of gas a month from two pumps. There would be five or six cars or more lined up at the pumps from morning 'til night, and tourists would be pouring into the station on foot faster than you could count them.

I had three people working at all times. Jana, Buddy and Kim also helped out. We added a walk-in cooler in the back to store cold beer, but still we couldn't keep our five drink boxes full of cold beer. Things were moving so fast, we quit using the cash register and just threw money in a cardboard box under the counter.

I don't think we ever kept an accurate tally of the money coming in. That was just the start of my bookkeeping problems with the IRS. I should have known better, but I ran the station for fun, not as some big business enterprise.

* * *

Frances Irlbeck, Billy's one-time private secretary, says, "If Billy had all the money today that he took in at the filling station, he'd be a rich man. He could have made even more money, but he was always giving things away."

Billy's son-in-law Mark Fuller, who leased the station from Billy from 1979 to 1981, says the cash register and cardboard box at the service station "were like a piggy bank to everyone. If Mr. Billy or Ms. Sybil or one of the kids needed some money, they'd just reach and take what they needed. No accounting, nothing.

"Mr. Billy was that way. He was generous to a fault. An awful lot of people took advantage of that. Some people started on their way up through his generosity, just as he was starting on his way down."

* * *

The regulars kept coming around to the station despite all the hub-bub. For the most part, they'd just ignore things.

Mr. Jack Pugh would just turn his back to people or a camera and just go on talking to his friends. We'd egg Mr. Jack on and beg him to talk to a reporter and have his picture taken. Finally, he'd tell us to go to hell and turn his back on us, too.

Mostly, we just did a lot of crazy stuff at the station.

One time Randy took off all his clothes and rode around naked in the freezing weather on Buddy's motorcycle to win a bet. Sybil was driving along when she saw Buddy's motorcycle streak by with this bare butt sticking up. She said she about died until she figured out it was Randy, not Buddy.

Funny thing was the motorcycle died a couple of times, and Randy had trouble getting it kick-started. There he was trying to kick start the motorcycle and cussing up a blue streak in the middle of Plains. All he had on was a pair of boots and a ski mask.

We could see the whole scene from in front of the station, and we were standing there laughing like hell and yelling at him.

Another time someone drove off in Bud Duvall's pick-up while he was inside the station. Bud was fit to be tied. He loved that pick-up more than he loved anything.

Bud found his pick-up and the guy a little later and came storming back into the station ranting and raving.

He said, "That no good son of a bitch not only had my pick-up, but he was wearing my favorite cap and had my checkbook sticking out of his back pocket. I wanted to kill him on the spot."

We also liked to play tricks on Chicken, the farmer we ran for State Senate. Chicken was always coming in to have a beer. Once, we hooked up a chain to the rear axle of his truck while he was drinking inside. Chicken didn't even notice when he got in the truck to leave. We heard him gunning the engine for a while, and finally he came back in and announced:

"Hell, I guess, I had better stay here and have a few more beers. Something's wrong with my truck."

* * *

You never knew what was going to happen at the station.

One time this wild band on its way to a $3000 gig down south of here stopped for some gas and a few beers and ended up picking, playing and dancing 'til three in the morning.

They missed their performance, but the guitar player told me, "To hell with the $3000. This was worth every penny of it."

* * *

The gas station was my campaign headquarters for my race for Mayor of Plains in 1976.

I ran against A.L. Blanton and lost by 19 votes. I lost all the Baptist and Methodist vote, and part of the Lutherans. I think they were paying me back for getting my beer license.

My campaign manager was Hogpen. He and I held a press conference at the gas station every morning with members of the national media. Later, Hogpen said he guessed we made a mistake running a national campaign, while Blanton was out rounding up the votes.

When Hogpen found out we had lost by 19 votes, he said, "Hell, Billy, if I had known it was going to be that close, I would have taken $100 and bought 20 votes for $5 apiece."

We spent a total of $7 on the campaign for a few "Billy Carter for Mayor" T-shirts, and several hundred dollars on an election party. Randy told me I wasn't worth a damn as a candidate, but I sure knew how to throw a party.

People were wall-to-wall at the party, but we counted only four eligible voters. Hogpen said no wonder we lost; we didn't have any friends who lived in the city limits.

* * *

It was fun running for mayor, and I sure didn't mind losing. But I wouldn't have minded winning, either.

I thought the town was going to hell in a basket. Out of towners were coming in and offering outrageous sums to legitimate merchants and setting up junk shops. They made their money and left, and today, downtown is nearly deserted because of them. We lost two grocery stores, a hardware store and several other businesses.

All we needed were some controls, but nobody was willing to take charge. I was head of the Merchants' Association for a while, but I didn't have any real power.

When things in Plains returned to normal in '82 or '83, I think people finally realized what they had lost. You had to drive 10 miles to Americus just to get a hand tool or a full order of groceries.

But, like I said, I didn't really mind losing the mayor's race. One politician in the Carter family was probably enough. Besides, I didn't have to keep any of the promises I made.

* * *

I've got to take time out to explain how my campaign manager Leon Johnson got the name "Hogpen."

I gave it to him when I was appearing on the Merv Griffin Show in Los Angeles. Merv asked me if there was any news from Plains, and I blurted out that Hogpen Johnson had run off the road between Americus and Plains and had "aborted" seven sows when he plowed into a hog farmer's farrowing pen. I said the farmer was suing Hogpen for $3 million.

The only truth in the story was that Leon had run off the road into a hogpen. I never had called Leon "Hogpen" before. It just came to me because I thought the nickname would make the story a little bit better.

Anyway, the name stuck.

Hogpen is a civil engineer from Georgia Tech who worked all over the world and retired in Plains after putting in a sewer system for the city. He said he decided to hang around to help me drink beer at the station.

Hogpen's one of the best I've ever seen at doing nothing. The other day, he and I went to breakfast, got some gas, picked up some cleaning, and went to Walmart to buy a coffee pot. We both decided we'd better take the next couple of days off to rest up after such a full day.

* * *

In the beginning, I thought all the excitement in Plains would die down once Jimmy was inaugurated and went to Washington.

I was wrong. It didn't matter to most tourists whether Jimmy was here or not. I guess I was good enough entertainment for most people. Finally, I decided to move Sybil and the kids to Buena Vista, about 20 miles north of Plains. People were walking up to our front door at all hours and following us everywhere we went. We couldn't get a moment's peace.

I was still in town a lot at the warehouse, but eventually I shifted my press headquarters to Jimmy Murray's Best Western Motel in Americus. It was really a better headquarters anyway; it had a full bar, which was always open to me.

The only difference when Jimmy was away in Washington is that most of the national media went with him. When they were in Plains or in Americus, where they stayed at the Best Western, they were always looking for a story. And when they couldn't find one, they came to me.

I liked Ed Bradley with CBS, and, like I said earlier, I got along fine with Sam Donaldson when he wasn't on camera.

One time, we were harassing Sam from the service station when he was doing a piece for the camera in the little park downtown. He messed up about four times, and just when he finally got it right, this big old mutt walked up behind him and did his business in full view of the camera. Sam finally gave up.

I realize the media had a tough job to do. They had to file a story everyday, and that's pretty hard to do in a little town like Plains. I was usually happy to feed them a little copy. It was fun at first, but then it got to be a pain.

No way, though, should they have been so dishonest in the way they went about getting stories. It would really make me mad when one of them would sit and drink with me for all hours and then turn around and do a story about my hard drinking. Other times, they would edit a story to show you in the worst light possible.

Even so, I think things kind of averaged out for me with the media. I never told them the truth when a lie would do just as well.

* * *

The media gave Jimmy holy hell.

One time Jody Powell (President Carter's Press Secretary) called me from Washington and asked if I could help beat back a story someone was doing on some black families living in sub-standard housing on our land.

It sounded like they wanted to make Jimmy out to be a slave owner or something. The Northern press never could get it through their heads that not all Southerners were bigots.

The fact was that Jimmy was letting the families live there free for as long as they liked.

I told Jody I would take care of it. I went out and found the families new places to live and burned the old houses to the ground.

Jody thanked me, but said I didn't have to go to such extremes. Anyway, nothing ever came of the story.

The Baptist Church thing in town was also blown way out of proportion. Someone from out of town forced the issue about the

Plains Baptist Church not admitting black members just to embarrass Jimmy.

I think Jimmy was really frustrated by all the race issue stuff. He was always having to prove he wasn't bigoted—instead of the other way around—all because he was a Southerner.

* * *

A couple of Jimmy's aides—I won't say whom—approached me for help on one other occasion.

I feel certain they never told Jimmy about it, and neither did I, until now.

The aides were concerned that Jimmy was coming across way too pious with all that born-again stuff. Jimmy had agreed to a *Playboy* magazine interview to try to soften his image, but his "lusting in his heart" statement just made matters worse.

They said they thought I would be a good counterbalance to Jimmy and asked me if I would mind pouring it on about religion.

I said, hell, since I felt that way honestly, it wouldn't be a problem.

I made some remarks I regretted later, but at the time, I didn't apologize for it. I never apologized for anything, right or wrong, until I got sober.

* * *

The only time the media and I were ever on the same side was in our softball games with Jimmy and his Secret Service Agents.

Those games were wild as hell. I think we outdrew the Atlanta Braves. People were sitting and standing everywhere at the old school ball field where we played.

Both sides would bring in ringers. We'd always notice these new agents coming into town right before a game. Jimmy had more strings to pull than we did, and, like I said, he had the umpires on his side, too.

In the middle of one game, my service station blew up. I ran like hell to get over there because I was afraid Buddy was in the station and that he and some others might be hurt.

As I was trying to get into the station, some photographer started blocking my way, and I just hauled off and hit him. When I came out, I jumped him again.

That night on the news all they showed was me hitting the photographer. It made me look like a fool. The media could be your friend one minute and turn on you the next.

But, finally, I said to hell with it. The night of the explosion, we had a big party at the station. I gave away 100 cases of beer.

That was life at the gas station. I'll wager you there will never be another gas station like that one.

CHAPTER THIRTEEN

When Plains started attracting attention in 1976 after it looked like Jimmy had the Democratic nomination wrapped up, things were still pretty routine for me.

The press focused on Mama for quite a while, and she kept them entertained. She was good copy.

I don't remember the first time I did a full interview with the press. Mostly, I did some short interviews to kind of flesh out stories people were doing on Jimmy or the whole family. Nothing special.

But when the media began to camp out in Plains after Jimmy was elected, things changed overnight. All of a sudden life was one big party to me.

I was ready to drink or shoot the bull with anybody, press and tourists alike. And if the press asked me about anything, I gave them some kind of an answer, even if I had to fake it. I don't think they were used to that, and they kept coming back for more.

I knew I was attracting a lot of national publicity, but still I wasn't expecting what came next.

Suddenly, I started getting offers from everywhere to appear at this and that. A lot of them promised the moon, but I didn't know how to separate a good offer from a bad one, or what to charge for an appearance. I couldn't believe people were willing to pay me big money for just showing up somewhere. It was too good to be true.

Finally, a friend recommended that I contact this agent, Tandy Rice, in Nashville, and he started handling my appearances.

The next two years were wild. I partied for almost two years straight, and enjoyed the hell out of it at first. But before it was over, I almost lost my marriage; I nearly killed myself drinking; and a lot of people, including some self-righteous U.S. Senators like Birch Bayh, were accusing me of things just short of treason.

Still, things weren't too bad on the average. I survived.

* * *

In 1977, Billy invited his future son-in-law Mark Fuller, a 22 year old college student, out to lunch and made him an unusual offer.

"I thought he was going to ask me to quit seeing Kim or something,"

Fuller says. "Instead, Mr. Billy offered me a $100 a day, plus expenses, to travel around the country with him and take care of all the details for him at promotional events, television shows, and the like. He said a lot of the other people out there claiming to have his best interests at heart were a lot of wormy bastards and that he wanted somebody he could trust with him.

"Mr. Billy was like that. Sometimes, he thought the only people he could trust were people from down home who he knew were loyal to him."

Fuller traveled with Billy for almost two years. He and the Carters' eldest daughter, Kim, whom he had been dating since 1976, were married in 1979, and he leased Billy's service station from 1979 to 1981.

Fuller says those two years on the road were an unbelievable whirlwind. "There were times when I felt guilty making all that money for really doing nothing, and other times, when I felt like there wasn't enough money in the world to pay me for what I was doing."

* * *

The things I enjoyed doing most in those two years were the nutty things, like the International Belly Flop contest in Canada, The 29-Cent Beauty Contest, Hollywood Squares, and the Hee Haw show.

I would have done any of those things for nothing. As it was, I was getting something like $5000 an appearance. I thought I had struck it rich, and I was spending money like it was water.

There was always a party going on, and the drinks were on me.

One time, I blew $13,000 at the tables in Las Vegas and probably would have blown more if I hadn't had to be somewhere else the next day. I was drunk as hell in Vegas and thought I was going to break the house.

Mark told me another time that our dinner tab one night was more than he had paid for his car.

A magazine printed a story that I was making a half million dollars a year, or more than twice what Jimmy was making as president. I denied that in print, but, for one year at least, it was true.

* * *

I also liked doing the TV talk shows. At one time, I think I held the record for the most appearances on the Donahue Show. Something like five or six times. I also enjoyed the Tom Snyder Show and the Merv Griffin Show.

CHAPTER THIRTEEN

I was in a T.V. movie, "Flat Bed Annie and Sweetie Pie." But movie making wasn't for me. I couldn't stand waiting around all day just to do one scene. It drove me crazy.

The talk shows were more to my liking, and the Merv Griffin Show was my favorite. Merv was real sincere and would always set you up for good lines and let you talk all you wanted. Once, though, I think I carried things too far for Merv.

Tom T. and I were in the audience when Mel Tillis was hosting the show for Merv, and we both decided Mel needed a little help. So we went up on the stage, uninvited Mel as the guest host and took over the show.

A few days later, I got a letter from Merv. All it said was:

"Billy, the next time you want to volunteer to help us out, don't. Merv."

* * *

Country and Western singer and composer Tom T. Hall and his wife Dixie became fast friends with Billy and Sybil in the mid-70s. Hall and Billy both had the same agent, Tandy Rice, of Nashville.

Dixie Hall vividly remembers her first introduction to the Carters.

"Tom T. had helped Jimmy in his campaign for governor in Georgia, and later he and Billy became acquainted when Billy came to Nashville to meet with Tandy. The day before I met Billy, I was listening to the radio and heard him and Sybil singing with Tom T. Billy couldn't sing a lick, but that didn't keep him from trying.

"Tom T. and Billy were very close, and Billy and I were kind of soul mates. I knew he had accepted me the first time he told me to 'kiss his ass.' Billy didn't kid around with people he didn't like.

"Later, Billy and I co-owned a black basset hound named 'Woody.' Billy said he wanted a dog, but couldn't keep one since his property wasn't fenced. Billy and I showed Woody at dog shows around the country, and he won a lot of ribbons. Billy and I had a lot of fun with him.

"I have a big interest in animals. We have an Animal Land near our home, where we take care of animals and train seeing eye dogs for the blind. We also maintain a wildlife preserve which we named in honor of Miss Lillian.

"One time Billy came up to me with a real serious look on his face and said:

'Dixie, I did you a big favor today.'

I asked him what it was, and he said:
'A dog urinated on my car, and I didn't kick him out of respect for you.'

* * *

I always liked to have a few of my friends around just in case things got a little dull on the road. That way I knew we'd always have a quorum for a party.

Hogpen was single then, so he was around a lot, and so was Randy Coleman.

One of the wildest parties we ever threw was during Jimmy's inauguration. We chartered a plane to Washington, and I rented a whole floor of a hotel.

We spilled out into the hallways and were raising so much hell that some of the guests called hotel security. When security got there, they found me, two senators and a couple of cabinet members sitting on the floor in the hallway drinking and playing poker. The head security guy just apologized and said he wouldn't disturb us again. I don't know what he told the guests who complained.

One of my friends showed up at the party with some girl in a short red dress with nothing on underneath. Capt. Brown of the Georgia State Patrol was there and was sitting on the floor when this girl walked by.

Capt. Brown usually just sat around, had a drink or two and didn't say too much. But I remember him looking up at this girl's bare butt and saying:

"Excuse me, Ma'am, but aren't you a little overdressed for this party?"

Late one night we all got hungry, and since we were tired of the room service menu, we collected some money and sent Randy out to get hamburgers.

Randy walked into an all-night hamburger joint, counted out $725 in small bills, and told them he wanted $200 worth of cheeseburgers, $300 worth of hamburgers, $75 in fries, and $150 in hot dogs.

* * *

Another big party was up in Utica, New York, where I was doing a snowmobile promotion for Billy Beer, which was brewed in Utica and several other places.

We partied for a couple of days. We had a snowmobile race, with pit stops at taverns every few miles along the way.

We got so drunk after a while that we couldn't find our way from one tavern to the next. We had a state patrolman with us, and he was just as drunk as we were. Once when we got lost, we ditched the snowmobile and jumped into a patrol car to go to the next tavern.

We roared up to this tavern with the sirens blaring and the lights flashing, and scared the wits out of everybody inside. It was the wrong tavern, and I think they were shooting craps or having a poker game inside.

We just joined them and invited them to come with us to the next tavern.

* * *

I talked some of my married friends into joining me from time to time. Finally, Don Carter told me if he hung out with me too much, he'd end up in divorce court.

Don always said I was the craziest S.O.B. alive, which must have meant he wasn't too particular about the company he kept.

Don is a commercial realtor up in Gainesville, north of Atlanta, and is chairman of the State Conservation Commission. When I was drinking, he was always on me about spoiling the environment by throwing beer cans out of my truck.

Don and I like pulling pranks on each other. One time, he paid this female impersonator $20 to come up and kiss me on the lips in a hotel bar.

Don's wife, Lucille, is real active in politics and was one of Jimmy's early supporters for governor. He and I met through politics, and not long after, he invited me up to his cabin in the mountains for some hunting and trout fishing.

I showed up with about 15 people and no rifles or rods. I said, hell, I was there to drink and play poker, not to hunt and fish.

About a year later, I invited Don down to Plains for a weekend of poker at the pond house. He showed up in this school bus full of people. Don would introduce me to the people as they got off at the front door of the bus, and then they'd circle back around through the back door and come off again.

I finally caught on when this guy named Klondike Bridges got off the second time.

Anyway, Don had 18 people with him, and they fleeced me good. I had to send Buddy back to the house to get some more money.

* * *

People were always trying to keep an eye on me while I was traveling, all the way back to the Democratic Convention in New York. At the convention, I began to notice that Walt Bellamy (the former Atlanta Hawk pro basketball player) always showed up everywhere I went.

Walt finally confessed to me that Jimmy's people had asked him to make sure I didn't get in any trouble while I was in New York. One time I came out of the hotel and insisted on joining a Gay Rights Parade which was coming down the street. Walt just kind of looked at me, and I backed off. I wasn't about to argue with Walt; he's one of the biggest human beings on the face of the earth.

I did manage to get into a parade at the Gator Bowl in Jacksonville, Florida. I got right in step with the Florida State Marching Band in the bowl game parade. Sybil had been looking for me all afternoon and was back at the hotel watching television when I appeared on the screen with the Florida State band. I think she could have killed me.

One time the watchdog act almost backfired on everyone.

I was to be the surprise guest at a salute to Liz Taylor in Los Angeles and was supposed to do a little routine with Bob Hope, which he and I had rehearsed the day before. Sybil, Mark and my agent Tandy were bound and determined I wasn't going to have anything to drink the day I went on.

I didn't realize it at the time, but I had reached the point in my alcoholism, where I couldn't go very long without a drink.

I had some gin stashed away at the hotel, but they wouldn't let me out of their sight when we went back to the hotel. I started becoming real nervous and agitated as the day wore on. Finally, just before I went on, Mark slipped me a tumbler of gin. I gulped it down, and everything came off fine.

If I hadn't had a drink, I think I might have gone into the DTs in the middle of the act.

Hope, though, probably would have made it seem like part of the act. I don't think anything would faze him.

* * *

My bread and butter on the touring circuit were big promotions for the opening of shopping centers built by Melvin Simon & Associates of Indianapolis, one of the top three or four shopping center developers in the country. It was a good pay day for me. A lot of my fees for the talk shows and other stuff hardly covered my bar bill. Most of them only paid union scale.

I hooked up with Mel Simon through Buck Sappenfield, Mel's national marketing director. He called the gas station one day looking for me. I told him he had to go through my agent in Nashville, but since he was a good ol' boy from Texas, we could probably do business together.

Generally speaking, I didn't want to work with people I didn't like, no matter how much it paid.

Working with me was probably the biggest mistake Buck ever made. I damned near ruined his career with my expense accounts, and damn near ruined his liver, too. One time I told Buck I needed to borrow his limousine in Dallas to go see my sister Ruth, who lived outside of Fort Worth at the time. He said, fine, but told me to watch the mileage because he was being charged $1.50 per mile. Ruth wasn't home, so some friends and I just drove around Dallas and Fort Worth all day long drinking beer in the backseat. I don't know how Buck explained the limo bill on his expense account. We drove around more than 500 miles and told the driver to give himself a big tip.

It's a wonder Buck survived the first time he and his family visited Plains. He said he just wanted to hang out with me and the boys while he was there, and I took him at his word. I would roust Buck out about six in the morning with a can of beer, and he would spend the rest of the day drinking with us.

One time at the station, Buck started drinking with a man we called "100 Proof" Williams. "100 Proof" broke the seal on a bottle, turned it up, drank about a third of the bottle without stopping and handed it to Buck. Buck's eyes were about as big as a saucer, but he hung in there until he almost passed out.

Finally, after about three days, Sybil rescued Buck and turned him over to his wife for safekeeping.

* * *

George (Buck) Sappenfield booked Billy Carter at six mall openings in '77 and '78. Billy always appeared with other celebrities and sports figures, but Sappenfield said Billy was usually the biggest draw at the event.

"Billy was something like a folk hero in those days. People related well to him. He was always willing to spend time with people. He would tease them, play with their kids, sign autographs, anything. It was hard to keep him on schedule.

"He would also do about anything you asked, as long as it was for charity. We would raise money for local charities at all of our openings. People would pay a fee, which went to charity, to participate in some event with a celebrity. I remember Billy getting all dressed up in white tie and tails to ride with people in a hot air balloon in Springfield, Illinois. The first time the balloon went up, I saw Billy peeking out over the side of the balloon basket in his white top hat, sipping vodka to keep his courage up.

"Before I met Billy the first time, I didn't know what to expect. I thought he might be a pretty shrewd operator and kind of difficult. Instead, I found him to be one of the warmest, most unaffected, unpretentious people I had ever met. He was very playful and always full of practical jokes, but when there was a job to be done, he did it.

"We became fast friends right off the bat and remained close the rest of his life. It struck me once that Billy never lost a friend. If you were his friend, you were his friend for life."

* * *

The one event I remember more than any at the shopping center openings was the time Buck had me crawl into the ring with Joe Frazier for one round in Longview, Texas.

They billed me as the "Plains Pounder" and said I was predicting a knockout of Frazier.

Before we got into the ring, it occurred to me that even a "love pat" from Frazier might be hard enough punch to break my jaw. Joe was one of the toughest boxers who ever lived. He used to soak his head in salt water before a fight to toughen up his skin. Before the fight, I went over to Joe's corner to check things out with Joe. He said he wouldn't hit me harder than I hit him and invited me to hit him as hard as I could. I damn near broke my hand, and he broke up laughing.

I enjoyed working with athletes. I worked with Rosey Grier, miler Jim Ryun, Lou Brock, Chris Evert, Kyle Rote, and Larry Mahan, the rodeo star. In Oklahoma City, Mahan, Rosey and I were billed as stars of "The Ramblin' Rodeo Review." Hogpen was there and sang our theme song, "Up Against the Wall You Redneck Mother."

I also became friends with Phil Niekro and Hank Aaron of the Atlanta Braves. Niekro was almost as old as I was and as out of shape and was still pitching. Niekro has a great sense of humor.

One year when the Braves were going bad, their owner Ted Turner asked me if I wanted to manage the team for one game. I told him, sure. They couldn't do any worse with me than they were already doing. The league office wouldn't let me do it, though.

Ted did manage the team himself for one game and caught all sorts of crap from the league.

* * *

I was always popping off for laughs, and it got me in trouble sometimes.

When I was in the ring with Frazier, I was supposed to taunt him. I yelled at Joe, "I'll fight you; I'll go to school with you; but I'll be damned if I'll eat with you at the same table tonight."

Joe thought that was funny as hell, but I got kind of worried that it might show up in print the next morning and get me in more hot water. Fortunately, it didn't.

* * *

I worked with a lot of show business people, too, and liked most of them—Bob Hope, Henry Winkler, Mary Ann Mobley, Clayton Moore (the Lone Ranger), and so on.

There was one guy, though, that I flat out couldn't stand. He had an ego the size of Texas and would complain if he didn't get top billing or star treatment one hundred percent of the time.

One time at a shopping mall opening, I happened to get to the best room in the hotel and couldn't resist rattling his cage about it. I went to his room, stepped it off, and told him my room was three or four feet wider. He complained about his accommodations the rest of the time we were there.

Another time he walked in barefoot to a party we were having, and I told him, "Damn, you've got the ugliest feet I've ever seen in my life." He just stormed out.

* * *

If I'm remembered for anything in my life—other than being Jimmy's wild young brother—it'll probably be for Billy Beer.

It's hard to believe now, but that stuff was only brewed for about a year. But it seems like everybody remembers it.

The funny thing was when Fall City Brewery in Louisville dreamed up the idea in 1978, I really wasn't drinking that much beer. I had graduated to the hard stuff, mainly vodka. I was always making a big deal about drinking beer to cover up my heavy vodka and whiskey drinking.

I had a lot of fun with Billy Beer, and the brewery treated me well. When I sobered up in 1979, they bought me out of my endorsement contract as a gesture. They didn't really have to, because by then, the beer's sales were dying anyway.

I have always taken a lot of pride in my honesty, so I still cringe when I see my endorsement on the Billy Beer can. I said, "It's the best beer I've ever tasted. Billy Carter."

That's a lie, of course. It was the worst stuff I had ever tasted. You had to be an alcoholic to drink it.

* * *

The Billy Beer taste probably wasn't the fault of the brewery. I chose it from about eight or ten formulas they had brewed for my inaugural taste test in Louisville.

Fact of the matter was I was so drunk when I got to Louisville for the taste test that they could have given me water in a glass and I wouldn't have known the difference.

The brewery had chartered a jet for me and my friends to fly from Plains to Louisville, and I had been knocking back vodka and grapefruit juice all the way there.

Anyway, after tasting all the batches, I finally just pointed at one and said that's the best. I don't know to this day whether the actual Billy Beer was the one I picked. But I prefer to take responsibility for it. I have trouble believing a reputable brewery would pick it.

* * *

Fall City Brewery, a small independent brewery in Louisville, K.Y., is no longer in business, but F.X. Matt Brewery in Utica, N.Y., which brewed Billy Beer for about three months in 1978, is now in its 101st year of operation.

F.X. Matt II, president of the family-owned New York brewery, says his company lost money on Billy Beer when sales suddenly took a nosedive a month or so into production.

"Distributors in New England started returning the beer to us by the caseload," Matt says, "and we were forced to discount it at a loss."

Matt, though, defends the quality of the beer to this day. "Billy joked about Billy Beer later, but I think he picked a good formula. He was a more sophisticated beer taster than he would care to admit.

"In fact, I think the beer got a bum rap. The media treated Billy Beer as a joke, but it was a good beer. It had a combination of three tastes—soft (a little on the light beer side) and hoppy, with a strong aftertaste. It was probably a little too sophisticated for American tastes."

Billy's swing through Utica to promote the beer was an unforgettable experience.

"When Billy arrived wearing cowboy boots and a big hat, all the women in the plant serenaded him with a song, 'Hello Billy,' which they sang to the tune of 'Hello Dolly.' He joined in and kissed all the women on the cheek—about fifteen of them in all. They were thrilled to death. I remember him being very warm and friendly. He was also one of the world's all-time great drinkers.

"All the people who went with him on the snowmobile race promotion in upstate New York almost died trying to keep up with him drinking. But they all had one heck of a time."

* * *

We had a Billy Beer Day in Plains when the beer was introduced. It was one of the wildest days ever in Plains. Everybody in town, except the Baptists, got drunk. People came from everywhere.

Jana got married about that time, and we had three boat loads of iced-down Billy Beer floating in the pool at our house.

We must have given away more Billy Beer in Plains than they ever sold. It's hard for me to believe that Billy Beer is a collector's item now. I guess people bought it to collect rather than drink.

If Billy Beer's worth what they say it is in a can ($500 a six pack), I must have made my friend Nookie Meadows a fortune. Nookie is a collector of beers from around the world, and as a gift to him, I had them bottle a few Billy Beers for him. As far as I know, those were the only bottles of Billy Beer ever produced.

* * *

Billy Beer wasn't my only endorsement. A toy car manufacturer came out with a Billy Carter "redneck pickup." That sold pretty well for a while, and I made a few bucks off it.

I also became a journalist. I bought the Plains Monitor and wrote a front page column for it for about six months. I also signed a contract with *Oui* magazine to write three columns for $20,000 each. I got around to writing one column on my favorite minister, Jerry Falwell, and I think they held their breath for a while to see if Falwell was going to sue.

I never could come up with an idea for my second column, but I don't think they really cared.

I bought the Monitor to try to chase Larry Flynt's rag out of town. My editor, Josh, whom I bought the paper from, was real good when he wasn't drunk. But when he was messed up, he would forget to put the paper out. He might not put out an issue for a couple of weeks.

Finally, I just gave the paper back to Josh.

* * *

There were a lot of good, crazy times for me for about 18 months.

During the peak of things, I hired Frances Irlbeck as my full time secretary just to keep up with correspondence and requests. We got hundreds of requests a day for autographed pictures, empty beer cans, peanuts and the like. People would also send in tapes of songs they had written about me.

There would be big piles of mail everywhere. Frances said she answered every letter. And I believe her. Our postage bill was larger than the national debt.

But in the fall of 1978, everything started to unravel because of my drinking and my finances. After that, it seemed like I got as much hate mail as I did fan mail.

CHAPTER FOURTEEN

In 1978, Donnie Roland, a close friend of Billy's and a partner in the Americus, Georgia, accounting firm which handled both Jimmy and Billy Carter's financial affairs, sent a certified letter to Billy warning him that his financial position was becoming precarious.

"I knew I was one of the only people he trusted on financial matters, and I felt obligated professionally and personally to write him a letter telling him that his problems with the IRS were only beginning and that he had to begin cutting back on his spending immediately," Roland says.

"It was nothing new to Billy. All of his close friends had tried to tell him to cut back. But I thought if he saw it written down in black and white, it may make an impact on him.

"Unfortunately, it had no impact. It seemed like things had to reach a point of desperation before Billy would do anything."

* * *

When I received that letter from Donnie, I knew he was right. It seemed like the wheels were coming off everything for me.

But I figured that I had come this far on my own terms and I may as well let things play themselves out. The money was still coming in, I was having a good time, and I damn sure wasn't going to give in to the IRS. I hated the IRS with a passion and was determined to fight them for every penny they said I owed them.

In my sane moments, when I was halfway sober, I would reason to myself that I had to do something about my finances, but after a few drinks, I would just say to hell with it.

Besides, finances weren't my worst problem. Drinking was. I wasn't capable of solving anything as long as I was drinking. That worried me at times, too, but the surefire cure for that was to drink some more.

One morning, when I was feeling real bad, I remember telling Mark (Fuller) that I couldn't live with the booze, and I couldn't live without it. I felt like throwing in the towel. But after a couple of drinks, I was feeling better and told Mark to forget what I had said. I told him I was just worn out.

* * *

I was exhausted from all the drinking, traveling and late nights. When I would get home, all I would do is sleep. Then I would be ready to go some more.

Even at my worst, though, I never seriously considered quitting drinking. That's why I didn't want to go to A.A. I knew the only way A.A. would work is if I gave up drinking altogether, and I wasn't ready to do that.

I thought if I could just cut back for a while, I could get straightened out. By then I was drinking half a fifth in the morning and about a half gallon a day. So I had a lot of room to cut back.

* * *

In 1978, Mark Fuller began to notice that Billy was drinking more and more and that he was becoming almost impossible to manage.

"When he was feeling bad in the morning, Mr. Billy would always say, 'Mark, I'm okay. I'm just worn out and pissed off.' One time, I said, 'Mr. Billy, it seems like you're worn out and pissed off a lot.' He looked at me real hard and told me to go to hell.

"Even before I took the job with him, I knew Mr. Billy drank a lot. But it was a big shock to me to find out just how much he drank. He drank from sunup to sundown, and I didn't know what to do about it.

"Toward the end, Mr. Billy was always threatening to pull out of a deal. All I could do was get him off by himself and let him cool down. The only way you could ever get Mr. Billy to do something was to convince him it was his idea.

"Once at an amusement park show, he was drunk and insisted that he wanted to be part of a dolphin show. This girl with the show told him it would be easy. She said the dolphin would jump up from the water and kiss Mr. Billy on the cheek. I told him it wasn't part of the deal, and he shouldn't do it. But he did it anyway, and this dolphin came out of the water, hit him right on the nose and knocked him over backward. His nose was sore for a long time after that.

"I thought it was funny as hell, and that maybe he would listen next time."

* * *

I was never without my booze. When I was leaving on a trip, I would always pack my tickets, a couple of half pints and cigarettes in my brief case.

Stewardesses on the airline would also load me down with miniatures on every flight. I always had enough miniatures to open a liquor store.

You might remember that Jimmy made a big deal about not serving hard liquor at the White House while he was president.

Still, the White House wasn't totally liquor-free. I knew where all the liquor was stashed. I remember once when I was there with Don Carter and some of the NASCAR race drivers, we raided the liquor cabinet in the back pantry.

Someone took a picture of us sitting out on a balcony with our feet propped on the railing and drinks in our hands.

I was at the White House several times, but I didn't always see Jimmy when I was there. You could kind of hide out back in the living quarters and not know if they were declaring World War III in the offices up front.

I stayed in the White House to hide from the press while I was in Washington for the Libyan hearings. I called first to see if I could stay, and Jimmy said, fine, as long as we didn't talk to each other. While I was there, Jimmy walked through a room where I was watching TV and never said a word, not even hello. I just kept on watching television.

* * *

On my first trip to Libya in September of 1978, our party flew in our own liquor since Libya is a dry country.

When I gave my deposition to the Senate Judiciary Committee, the Committee Counsel Joseph Barker kept asking me about my drinking in Libya. He asked me if I was ever "under the influence" in Libya, and I told him, no, but said that I got pretty gassed when I was in Rome on the way back.

He asked me if I drank the whole time that I was in Libya.

I said, "For a while."

"You did not continue to drink the whole time?"

I said, "No."

"Why not?"

And, I said, "We ran out."

A couple of years later, I saw Richard Pryor on the "Tonight Show" after he had quit drinking and using. Johnny Carson asked him how much he used to drink.

Pryor said, "'Til there wasn't no more."
That's the way it was with me.

* * *

That first trip to Libya finished me off on the second-rate celebrity tour, pure and simple.

When I got back, there were five cancellation notices for appearances waiting for me. Things just dried up overnight because of all the negative publicity. After that, the only income I had for the next couple of years was from the gas station and some residuals for some commercials and television shows I had done.

A lot of people had told me I shouldn't go, but, as usual, I didn't listen. When I was first approached about going right before July 4 by (State Senator) Floyd Hudgins of Georgia and some other people, I put them off. But, later, when they reassured me it was nothing but a goodwill trip, I agreed. I thought I needed a break from touring, and it might be a lot of fun. Too, I had always wanted to see that part of the world.

I kept quiet about it to Jimmy because I knew he would be opposed to the trip. He didn't find out about it until I was on my way to Rome. From all I hear, he was a hell of a lot less than pleased.

I was told that I could invite one other person, so I invited Don Carter. When Don decided not to go, I invited Randy Coleman.

* * *

Don Carter tentatively accepted Billy's offer to accompany him to Libya, but decided to call a friend in Atlanta with connections with U.S. State Department to seek his advice before firming up plans.

"He advised me not to go because of the strain in relations between the U.S. and Libyan governments," Don Carter recalls. "He also pointed out that Libya was considered the second most dangerous place in the world for U.S. citizens, behind Cambodia. He also urged me to try to convince Billy not to go.

"I drove down to Plains (about five hours away) to tell Billy of my decision and to try to talk him out of the trip. I remember sitting in his living room pleading with Billy. I said it wasn't in my best interest to go, and it damn sure wasn't in his best interest. Sybil was crying and pleading with Billy, too. But he wouldn't budge.

"I remember him saying if Libya was as dangerous as they said, then he sure as hell wanted to go for the adventure.

"I never considered calling Jimmy or anyone else. I thought if I couldn't

influence Billy on this, nobody else could. I kept hoping up until the last minute that he might reconsider, but I should have known better. He was too damn stubborn."

* * *

There wasn't much to the first trip. We were in Libya four or five days and went to a lot of receptions and toured around a little. My favorite part of the trip was seeing the agriculture. I talked to some Libyan farmers and really didn't think they were much different from Georgia farmers except for the language and the farm equipment they used. They didn't wear overalls, either.

All my expenses were paid, but I didn't make a penny off the trip. They gave me a few souvenirs, which were valued at about $400 for tax purposes. In fact, I lost $5000 because I had to cancel a promotional appearance to clear my schedule.

People seem to think the trip was my idea. Nothing could be further from the truth. I didn't know Libya from Liberia until Hudgins and the others first talked to me in July of '78 at the gas station. I understood that the trip was to be a goodwill trip organized by (Ahmed) Shahati of Libya to help develop trade between our country and theirs. And nothing happened on that first trip to make me think it was anything other than that.

One thing really hit home for me, though. Libya was importing almost all of their food, and exporting almost all of their oil. Since we were doing just the opposite in America, it didn't make much sense to me that we weren't willing to work with them. I told Jimmy what I thought several times, but he never responded. He wasn't about to get drawn into a discussion of Libya with me, even informally.

Looking back, I can see I might have been pretty naive about the whole thing. But back then I was drunk most of the time, and I was determined to do what I damned well pleased, even if my brother was president.

It would have been a miracle if I hadn't made a stupid decision. Have you ever known a drunk who used good judgment?

* * *

When all hell broke loose on my return from Libya, I did what any self-respecting drunk would do. I dug in and started drinking even more.

I also begin to think that working with the Libyans was my only salvation. If they wanted to establish trade with U.S. companies, I would see what I could do to help them. I didn't have anything else to do except hang around the station.

I quit talking to the press. A lot of them were still okay, like my friend Clarence Gibbons with CBS and a few others. But the Northern liberal press was crucifying me. The worst offenders were (columnist) Jack Anderson and William Safire of the New York Times. I couldn't believe all the stuff Anderson wrote. He and his so-called reliable sources weren't anywhere near the truth.

I did one more shopping center opening with Buck, completed my commercial deal for Billy Beer and did a few more odds and ends. But basically from October to December of 1978, I didn't do anything but drink.

* * *

I acted as a host of sorts to a Libyan trade delegation that came to the United States for a 13-day visit in January 1979, but by then, I was in a fog because of my drinking.

I began having memory blackouts for the first time in my life, and I quit eating altogether because I couldn't hold food on my stomach. I threw up every time I tried to eat. Before I went into the hospital for detox, I hadn't eaten a regular meal for 58 straight days.

One time at dinner in a restaurant, Buck Sappenfield kept insisting I eat something. Finally, I told the waiter, "Okay, bring me one of every item on the menu." I'll be damned if he didn't bring what I ordered. Buck got stuck with a check for several hundred dollars. Still, I couldn't force myself to eat. I just ordered more to drink.

I had reached the point, too, that if I went more than a few hours without a drink, I'd start shaking so badly that I couldn't hold a glass. I'd been jump starting myself for two years — first with beers, then a half-pint of vodka, then a pint. I had to drink my vodka warm just to hold it on my stomach in the morning.

Still, I didn't think I was an alcoholic. I thought I was just going through a bad time, and that I could cut back when things smoothed out.

There was a hell of lot of insanity around me, and I thought the only way I could survive was by drinking. It never occurred to me that I was the cause of the insanity.

* * *

I kept getting into arguments and fights, too, which some people thought was unbecoming to a 42-year-old father of six.

I started a near riot in Birmingham. I was with Randy Coleman, Randall Woodruff, and Bill (Daddy Bear) Woodruff. A dentist and his son were in the same bar, and they kept walking by and calling Jimmy a son of a bitch.

Finally, I just stood up and hit the dentist. All hell broke loose. I remember Daddy Bear swung a chair and knocked a chandelier down on his head. We barely got out ahead of the police.

When I was drunk, I thought I could whip anybody.

* * *

The one thing that got me into the most trouble, though, was my mouth.

After the Libyans had visited Atlanta, we went up to New York.

I had decided not to talk to the press, but I was getting raked over in the press anyway. While we were waiting for the Libyans to land in Atlanta, I had taken a leak on the runway outside the car. We'd been in the car a couple of hours, and I couldn't hold it anymore.

The next day this reporter, who had done the same thing, wrote about my taking a leak on the runway. I could have killed him.

Anyway, at a reception for the Libyans at the Waldorf-Astoria, I finally caved into the badgering of the press. Some radio guy had managed to get into the reception with his equipment, and he kept jamming the mike in my face and asking me what I thought about Jewish opposition to my connections with the Libyans.

I told him there were a hell of a lot more Arabs than Jews in the world.

Mark and Randy whisked me away from the guy, but it was too late. That was what the media had been waiting for. They plastered that quote all over the world. Even Jimmy made a strong point of dissociating himself from that remark.

I didn't retract what I said, or apologize for it. What was the use? Besides, I was too drunk at the time to care what I said. It's a wonder I didn't hit the guy.

After that, I retreated to Plains and tried to stay out of sight as best I could. I was exhausted, and I was sick as hell with bronchitis and a bleeding stomach. But I kept right on drinking up until the time I entered the hospital.

* * *

Billy's friends viewed his constant drinking with concern and tried on a number of occasions to intervene with him. Each time, he refused to listen.

Doug Unger, a close friend for whom Billy once obtained an impossible-to-get loan for a land purchase, recalls that Billy began drinking "non-stop" when he was traveling in 1978.

"I was with him at the "All Star Anything Goes" show in Nashville when he appeared with Jerry Lee Lewis," Unger says. "Billy got so drunk we had to carry him away. Not long after that, in the spring of 1978, I picked up Billy and Tom T. (Hall) in Atlanta and took them to a concert in Gainesville. Billy was already drunk, and later that night, he passed out at someone's house.

"Tandy Rice and I went to pick him up, and Tandy asked me to talk to him. He thought maybe Billy would listen to me. I tried then, and I tried again later. Billy told me he'd like to cut back on his drinking, but he didn't know whether he could. He was just putting me off.

"I was thrilled when Billy finally decided to get help. He couldn't have made it very much longer."

* * *

Another close personal friend who was concerned about Billy's drinking and overall health was Dr. Paul Broun, the Carter family physician. Finally, on February 22, 1979, after a year of trying to bag his elusive quarry, Dr. Broun succeeded in convincing Billy to enter Sumter County Regional Hospital in Americus.

The diagnosis was bronchitis.

"I knew I couldn't persuade Billy to go to the hospital for his drinking, so I looked for another medical reason," Dr. Broun recalls. "His acute bronchitis finally gave me the opportunity I was looking for. He was a very sick man. After I had Billy where I wanted him, I told him:

"'Billy, I'm going to treat your bronchitis and your bleeding stomach, but first I'm going to detox you whether you like it or not.

"I had tried twice before to admit him to the hospital for detox, but failed both times. He was surprisingly healthly in the first physical I gave him, and he was showing only minimal effects of smoking and drinking in the second one.

"Billy had always been a very poor patient. He was difficult to tie down. Even when I made the diagnosis of bronchitis, he reacted by making a bunch of jokes. He said if he had known he was sick, he would have gone to a real doctor. Billy was always telling people my M.D. stood for 'Mexican Degree.'

"I began to see there wasn't much time to waste when I flew over to

Louisiana to join him for the Cajun music festival. When I got in the car at the airport, Billy had a six-pack of beer on either side of him and proceeded to drink all 12 cans on the way to our hotel. A little later, I went with him to the Hee Haw Show in Nashville, and he drank vodka all the time I was with him. I tried to talk to him both times, but he wouldn't listen.

"I think Billy thought he was going to sail through detox and get me off his back. But he was in for a great shock."

CHAPTER FIFTEEN

Detox was pure hell.

I had heard about the DTs (delirium tremens) and about thinking spiders and insects were crawling all over you, but there ain't no way in hell to prepare for the DTs. Seeing is believing. I thought I was going crazy, and Sybil thought I was dying. Given a choice, I think I would have picked dying.

Dr. Paul was surprised, too, by how bad my withdrawal was. It wasn't his fault, though. I never did exactly level with him about how much I had been drinking. I was afraid he would think I was an alcoholic and want to lock me up somewhere.

* * *

When Dr. Paul told me he was going to detox me, I didn't bat an eye. I knew beforehand there wouldn't be any booze in the hospital, so I had stashed four pints of vodka in my things.

After I was all alone that first night in the hospital, I got up to get a pint from my luggage. All four pints were gone. They had searched my luggage. I started to get a little concerned at that point.

The first couple of days weren't too bad, though. The IV tubes and stomach pump made me nervous, but mostly, I slept all the time. Still, I was already making plans to leave. I thought the bed rest would halfway restore me, and once they unhooked me from the IVs, I'd get my clothes on and walk out.

On the third day, everything turned upside down.

I went berserk. The nurses came to look at my room as a battle zone. People told me I'd pull out my IV and throw it at the nurses and that I'd cuss them out unmercifully every time they entered the room.

When I was leaving the hospital, I was too embarrassed to look any of the nurses in the eye. And, I don't embarrass easy.

For five or six straight days, I didn't get a moment's peace.

I was shaking like a leaf.

I was sweating like a pig.

I didn't recognize people in the room with me, even Sybil and the children.

I threw up from morning to night.

And, sure enough, I saw spiders and ants and bugs of every size and shape and strange-looking people. Once, I remember seeing the devil sitting on the window sill. He was laughing like hell at me. Finally, I threw something at him.

It was awful. I thought I was going crazy. I didn't begin coming around until about the eighth day. By then, I was mentally and physically exhausted and as edgy as a cat.

Those eleven days in the hospital were easily the worst experience of my life. Nothing in all my cancer treatment—the surgery, the chemotherapy, the Interleukin-2 treatment—held a candle to detox.

You hear how bad withdrawal from heroin and other drugs is, but I'm here to tell you they ain't nothing compared to alcohol — not if you'd been drinking like I had.

They ought to quit concentrating on illegal drugs all the time and make every kid look at a film of somebody in alcohol detox. Maybe they could use an ex-athlete and get Miller Lite to sponsor it.

I can't believe how old-time A.A. people used to detox on honey and Karo syrup. It's a wonder any of them lived to tell about it.

Still, when the shakes finally ended, the first thing that popped into my mind was:

"I'm clean now. I can start in drinking fresh."

* * *

Billy's detox was a nightmare for Dr. Broun, too. Not only did he have to contend with a difficult case, he had to contend with the media as well.

"The press was camped out in Americus. They followed me everywhere I went, even down to some bird-dog trials in Albany. I stuck with my story that Billy had been admitted for severe bronchitis and deflected questions about his alcoholism. It was up to Billy to tell the press about his drinking.

"Sybil was scared to death, too. She was afraid Billy might die from the seizures, and she didn't know what to do next. It was a very, very difficult situation for her to deal with.

"I knew that detox wasn't enough for Billy—that he needed rehabilitative treatment. I called President Carter and enlisted his support. I told Jimmy that Billy had a very severe alcohol problem."

President Carter discussed the situation with the White House Physician (Admiral Bill Lukash), and they made arrangements for Billy to enter the alcohol rehabilitation program at Long Beach Naval Hospital in California, which was generally regarded as one of the premier treatment programs in the country at the time. Alumni included former First Lady Betty Ford, Sen. Herman Talmadge, a fellow Georgian, and Astronaut Buzz Aldrin.

President Carter, as Commander-in-Chief of the Armed Forces, reactivated Billy in the Marine Corps to make him eligible for admission to the military hospital.

* * *

Capt. Joseph Pursch, the dapper, Yugoslavian-born chief of the Alcohol Rehabilitation Service at Long Beach Naval Hospital, was watching television in the Officer's Club at a Naval installation in Hawaii when he heard the news that Billy Carter had been admitted to the hospital for "severe bronchitis."

"I thought severe bronchitis, my eye," Dr. Pursch recalls. "I didn't know Billy at the time, but I knew by his exploits that he was probably an alcoholic. I had thought privately that it was just a matter of time before he went into the hospital or drank himself to death.

"When I got back to Long Beach, I called Admiral Lukash at the White House and told him I thought we could help Billy if they could get him to us. He agreed and said he would talk to the president about it."

The stage was set, but the trick was convincing Billy to enter treatment.

* * *

Dr. Broun and Sybil both talked to Billy about entering treatment, but he was either non-committal or outright resistant.

"Finally, after talking to Jimmy several times, we all agreed to ask Bert Lance (President Carter's first Budget Director) to come down to talk to Billy," Dr. Broun says. "Billy probably respected Bert Lance more than he did anyone else in the world, and we thought maybe Bert could convince him to go into treatment.

"Bert talked to Billy at length and told him that he agreed wholeheartedly with Sybil's and my opinion and wanted him to at least give treatment a try.

"I'm not sure Bert totally convinced Billy, but he succeeded in getting him to consider it."

* * *

I didn't want to go into alcoholism treatment after leaving the hospital in Americus. But I finally agreed to go because I was tired as hell, and I felt like I needed a place to hide out from the media. I wasn't up to all the badgering about Libya.

Nobody ever mentioned that they had arranged for me to go to

Long Beach, so I did a little research of my own on a good place to go. I talked to some friends, and one of them mentioned a place in Houston where they didn't preach giving up alcohol for good. That sounded pretty good to me, so I started talking up that place. After learning to become a social drinker in Houston, I thought it might be nice to slip out of the country for a while and meet up with some friends in Venezuela.

I thought I had sold everybody on Houston, so I started getting ready to go.

I kept my long-range plans to myself, but Sybil became a little suspicious when I asked her to pick up my passport before I left. I told her I just didn't feel comfortable anymore traveling without a passport.

I also took a pre-paid ticket to London with me. I figured that I could cash the ticket in to get extra cash.

Once I had my escape plans made, I just sat back and relaxed. I was surprised when they told me on the way to the airport in Atlanta that I was going to Long Beach. But I figured what the hell—I could get to Venezuela from Long Beach, too.

Still, I thought for awhile about jumping ship at a stop in Houston. But Sybil was with me, and a couple of guys from Eastern Airlines even went with me into the rest room. They made out like they were trying to shield me from the public.

* * *

On the flight out, a stewardess whom I had flown with before brought me out two miniatures of gin right after take off.

I turned them down. It was the first time in my life I had ever turned down a drink.

* * *

Dr. Bill Griffith, the Long Beach physician assigned to my case, met Sybil and me at the airport in Los Angeles and took us to Long Beach. I didn't know at the time that Sybil would be staying for family treatment, and neither did she. I hadn't figured on that in my escape plans.

The Naval hospital is on the grounds of a Naval base, and when we went through the gate on the base, it made me feel like I was going to prison. It was depressing as hell. The only good thing about it was that I knew the media couldn't get at me on the base.

CHAPTER FIFTEEN

I knew a little about what to expect in treatment, but really hadn't paid too much attention to details because I had no intention of staying very long or cooperating.

I didn't cooperate in the beginning, but the psychologists and counselors made it damned hard for me not to. Treatment consists of a lot of group therapy and lectures, and I made up my mind early on that I wasn't going to say a word in group therapy.

The counselors kept trying to draw me into the group discussions, and we ended up in a couple of shouting matches. Once I just said to hell with all of you and left.

They also kept hammering away at me to admit that I was an alcoholic, but I never did. I would always say I was just a heavy drinker.

I was in a four-man room, and I talked quite a bit with the other patients, but I was leery of the staff and thought the whole damned program was ridiculous.

We were supposed to talk about ourselves and our feelings in a room full of military officers, Marine Corps privates, seamen and the like. There was even a Vice Admiral in one of the groups. I had never talked about feelings before and wasn't about to start then. I thought they were trying to brainwash me.

The first staff person I begin to feel like I could trust was my counselor Mike Brubaker. He was as stubborn as I was and had quit drinking a few years earlier. I began to think if Brubaker could quit drinking, I could, too.

* * *

I raised so much hell with Dr. Pursch about the treatment that he farmed me out to a private hospital for a couple of days just to prove to me that the Navy program was about the same as those at private hospitals.

He said the Houston program I had heard about was just a myth.

Once I was in Dr. Pursch's office for a session when his phone rang. When he answered and started talking on the phone, I stormed out. I told him if he couldn't give me all of his attention, then I sure wasn't going to give him mine.

* * *

Mike Brubaker, a gregarious 49 year old retired Navy veteran, was a perfect match for Billy. He was as verbose and combative as his celebrated patient. Brubaker recognized from the beginning Billy didn't want to be in treatment and worked hard to earn Billy's trust.

"Billy was a difficult patient," Brubaker recalls. "I knew he didn't want to quit drinking, and that he was here more or less out of compliance.

"I learned quickly that he wasn't the buffoon he made himself out to be with the media. He was a bright guy with a great sense of humor. He could carry on a conversation about almost anything under the sun. I also recognized that underneath all his bluster, he was a sensitive, kind of shy person.

"At the time Billy came to us he was tired of being in the public eye and didn't trust anyone. I think the reason he and I got along so well was that he knew I was honest with him.

"I told him he was a drunk just like the rest of us, and that he had to get sober the same way we did.

"Billy confided in me that he was planning to bolt as soon as possible and that he had an airline ticket to London with him. I talked him into letting me hold the ticket for him. I said if he ever wanted it, all he had to do was come to me and I would give it to him.

"After about three weeks, Billy asked me to mail the ticket to Randy Coleman in Plains for him to use. I knew then we were heading in the right direction.

"For a long time, I think the only two people in the world who thought he would stay sober were him and me."

* * *

The truth of the matter is that in the beginning at Long Beach, I was feeling sorry for myself.

I felt like everyone in the whole world—including my wife — had done dumped on me. I felt like they had packed me off to Long Beach just to get me out of their hair.

And I felt sorry for myself because I wasn't getting any special attention. I was being treated like any other drunk off the street.

I didn't really realize all this about myself until about a year after treatment when I came back out to Long Beach for Joe Pursch's retirement party. It struck me then how difficult I had been as a patient.

All those people—Pursch, Brubaker, Bill Griffith, Ed Owen (another counselor) and the other patients—had helped me in spite of myself.

I also realized that I would have been dead without treatment. A lot of people get sober with A.A. alone. But I wasn't one of them. I needed treatment.

* * *

After about the third week in treatment—when most patients are getting ready to go home — I finally realized that I needed to be there.

If there was a moment of truth for me, it came in a family counseling session with Sybil. Sybil said if I wanted to keep on drinking, that was my business. She said she loved me, but that she and the kids could look out for themselves.

It made me mad at first when she said that, and then I felt hurt about it. But, finally, I thought, by God, if Sybil can change like that, I can, too. I would show her.

After I started listening and not raising hell, the things people were saying started making sense to me. I still wasn't too good about sharing my feelings, but I was beginning to get a pretty good idea of what it took for me to stay sober.

I also began to relax a little. I went out to play golf with Brubaker on the Navy course a few times and began going to A.A. meetings with Mike and the others. It was nice for a change to go places where I wasn't bothered by the press.

I knew I was going to have to face a lot of stuff when I got out of treatment, and I really started to dread leaving. I was there so long (seven weeks) that I think some people started to think I was a member of the staff. I must have outlasted about a dozen roommates.

Like I've always said, I'm a slow learner.

* * *

Joe Pursch thought the best way for me to handle my discharge from treatment was to hold a press conference at the hospital.

There had been some controversy over me entering a government treatment program. Some people didn't think the government should foot the bill for my treatment and raised a lot of hell about it. I also got a lot of hate mail while I was in treatment, but Dr. Pursch screened my mail and didn't let me see the negative stuff until a long time after I had been discharged. I just saw the cards and letters offering me encouragement.

Dr. Pursch said that with a press conference, I could get all the questions over with at once, and that he would be there to help me over the rough spots. He told me, though, that he wanted me to acknowledge my alcoholism right off the bat.

So I started out by saying I was alcoholic. It was the first time I had ever admitted aloud that I was an alcoholic.

* * *

As much as I worked at staying sober, it took me about three years after treatment to learn how to live sober.

My sobriety was what people in A.A. call a "white knuckler." I was not drinking on determination alone, and my life wasn't getting much better.

I finally quit blaming people and things for all the junk that had happened to me and learned to take responsibility myself.

It also took me three or four years to become comfortable with not drinking. At first, I was ashamed not to be drinking, and for a long time, I felt naked in public without a drink in my hand. Hard drinking had been a big part of the act I put on in public. I think Dr. Pursch, Brubaker and Dr. Griffith all realized it was going to be tough for me, and they kept up with me a little closer than they did most of their patients.

One time Pursch, who's kind of a fitness nut, came down to visit us in Georgia and got up early one morning to go jogging. He came running back up our driveway, which was real steep, a couple of minutes later with a dog after him.

I told him, "Joe, you ain't in California. Our dogs aren't used to guys running around in jogging suits."

Brubaker also stops by from time to time to visit with me and Herman Talmadge, who lives up near Atlanta. All Brubaker ever wants to do is play golf and go to A.A. meetings. He thinks he's one of the world's great golfers and insists on dragging me along with him. The strongest part of my golf game is dredging for balls in the water.

* * *

For the first five years I was sober, I didn't make too big a deal of it in public.

I flat out just didn't think I was strong enough in my own recovery to go around talking about how I got sober. Hell, I did everything wrong in the beginning.

I was always willing to help people one-on-one, but I thought I should leave the speaking to the pros.

Finally, people convinced me that I ought to start speaking because a lot of people might identify with me. They also convinced me it would strengthen my own sobriety.

The first time I spoke in public was on an alcohol awareness program. I was surprised how well I was received.

Damned if I don't think I've helped a few people since then. It kind of makes up for how bad a patient I was at Long Beach.

* * *

Dr. Joseph Pursch says without reservation that Billy Carter was one of his favorite patients.

"Billy is a textbook example of what treatment can do for a person," Dr. Pursch says. "He was in terrible shape when he got to us. He was in bad health—bloated, pale and exhausted—and he was in total denial about his problem.

"I'll never forget how the press reacted when Billy came out to meet them after seven weeks of treatment. He was cheerful, pleasant and a picture of good health. I don't think the press could believe how he had changed.

"The thing I am proudest of, though, is how Billy has helped so many other people with problems. Rarely, a week went by in his nine years of sobriety that he or Sybil didn't help someone. I always knew I could count on Billy, day or night, to drop what he was doing and call someone I thought he could help.

"Billy was an original."

CHAPTER SIXTEEN

Sybil

I never knew what to expect from Billy.

I was very nervous the first time I went to visit Billy in detox. I didn't know how he would react. But when he saw me, he started to cry. He said he didn't think I would come to see him because he was an alcoholic. He said he was afraid that I would leave him.

I said, "Sugar, I knew you were an alcoholic long before now, and I'm glad you're here."

Later, after I had all but given up hope that he would go into alcoholism treatment, Billy told me that he had decided he was going.

I didn't take him seriously at first. Billy had promised 100 times before that he was going to do something about his drinking, but he never had. He had broken promises to me, to Dr. Broun, to his friends. I didn't think he wanted to stop drinking, or even cut back.

But after he started making plans on what to pack, it gradually began to dawn on me that he was actually going. I couldn't believe it.

The final surprise for me came when he decided to stay at Long Beach. I had heard him fuss around for days about how he hated the place and how they were just playing games with him. I didn't know about the ticket to London and his plot to slip off to South America, but still I didn't expect him to stay in treatment.

Usually, if Billy decided he didn't like someone or something, nothing could change his mind.

After three weeks in family treatment myself, I found that I didn't care whether Billy stayed or not. I told Billy that I cared for him and loved him, but it was up to him whether he completed treatment. I told him that I would be fine whatever he decided. Billy was shocked, and to tell the truth, so was I. I was so used to agreeing with Billy and trying to save his feelings that it was hard for me to pull away.

But I was determined I wasn't going back to the way things were before.

* * *

The last couple of years before Billy went into treatment had been a nightmare for me.

At first, when Billy began to attract attention, everything had been exciting. Still, I couldn't understand why people thought Billy merited so much attention and why they were willing to pay him for appearances.

I did a lot of interviews myself on what it was like being part of the Carter family and being married to Billy. I enjoyed the interviews. It was the first time I had ever had an opportunity to express my feelings and thoughts.

Yet, I felt like all this was happening to someone else. It never felt real to me. I was used to Jimmy being well-known, but not us.

The first real intrusion for us was the lack of privacy we had in Plains. I became worried about the kids' safety. Contrary to what a lot of people think, the president's brothers and sisters and their families don't receive Secret Service protection. We had to fend for ourselves.

When we moved to Buena Vista, things leveled out some for me and the kids. Earl was a baby, and I spent most of my time working at the new house. I enjoyed our home. We added a new wing to the house and built a swimming pool.

It was like a dream world for me. We had more money than we ever had before, and Billy didn't restrict my spending on the house.

Billy was just starting to travel, and that was fine, too—at first. He was enjoying himself, and I was content with that. But before long, I found out that he didn't want me included in that part of his life.

* * *

I went with Billy on some trips in 1977, but I began to feel like a fifth wheel. People would look at me as if to say, "Who are you?"

Billy didn't go out of his way to make me feel welcome. He never told me I couldn't come along, but I began to realize he didn't want me there. If I weren't there, he could drink as much as he wanted, say what he wanted and do what he wanted.

After Jimmy was first elected, Billy delighted in giving crazy answers to questions from the national press. I thought it was funny for awhile, but he began to get carried away with it when he was traveling and making personal appearances.

He did a lot of unnecessary things. He cursed a lot for shock value and made a lot of crude or rude remarks just to be outrageous.

Billy would always make excuses to me for his behavior. He would say, "That's what they pay me to do," and laugh it away.

I finally reached the point where I didn't want to be associated with any of that activity. It just wasn't worth it to me.

* * *

Things weren't much better when Billy was home. He was tired and irritable when he was at the house, and everybody had to be at his beck and call.

He spent what spare time he did have out drinking with his friends at the gas station or at the Best Western Motel in Americus.

We also had a lot of parties at our home. The parties were a mixed bag for me. I enjoyed the new friends we had made, and enjoyed having them in our home. But Billy was drinking so much, it seemed like we couldn't enjoy our friends together. We were growing apart, and there wasn't much I could do about it.

Billy was going to do what he wanted to do regardless of what I said. The few times I did try to talk to him about our relationship, he acted like I was being a nag and wasting his time.

During that period, my dad died.

My dad and I were real close, but because of all the hub-bub around us, I never felt like I had the chance to mourn his death.

Jana Kae also got married during that period. It should have been a joyous occasion, but it was fraught with confusion and turmoil, just like the rest of our life.

I enjoyed planning for the wedding, but it rained on the day of the wedding, and the party at our house afterward turned into a nightmare. People we barely knew showed up, and they were stealing silverware and everything that wasn't tied down for souvenirs.

I thought we were spending too much for the wedding, but Billy told me not to worry. That's the way he was at that time. He never put any limits on anything, including himself.

I know now that he was exhibiting classic alcoholic behavior, but I didn't know it at the time. He was very grandiose in all aspects of his behavior.

* * *

Matters got progressively worse in the last year of Billy's drinking. Billy was drinking so much and gone so much of the time, it reached the point where I was glad when he was gone. I think the kids were, too.

I was embarrassed a lot of the time and was always make excuses for Billy to the children and our friends.

A number of times, Billy promised to be home for some special occasion for the kids, but he never made it. He missed their birthdays, holidays and so on.

The worst time was when he was supposed to escort Marle at her coronation as Homecoming Queen at the high school. He called at the last minute and said he couldn't make it. I could tell he was drunk when he called. Marle was crushed, but she never complained to me or her dad.

I had to ask our friend, Nookie Meadows, to stand in for Billy and spent the whole night making excuses for him.

I gradually became a nervous wreck. All the lies and broken promises took a toll on me. I couldn't sleep. It was like everyday had become a nightmare.

* * *

I knew Billy was drinking a lot, but I had no idea that he was up to a half gallon a day, plus beer.

The first hint I got was when I heard through a friend that someone had observed Billy drinking a whole bottle of vodka or gin one morning in his hotel room.

This is the way the story went. Billy was still asleep, with an unopened bottle next to him, when this friend left for a morning meeting. When the friend returned about three hours later, Billy was up and about drinking a beer, and the new bottle was completely empty.

I had trouble believing that he was drinking that much, but I found out later that was routine for him.

I finally resigned myself to the fact that Billy was going to drink himself to death.

The worst part was that I felt like I should have been able to stop it—and that somehow, some way I was responsible for it.

* * *

I was happy that Billy had decided to go into treatment at Long Beach, but I didn't let my hopes get too high.

I had been disappointed too many times before, like when he first tried A.A. about 20 years earlier.

But like a dutiful wife, I went with him on the plane to make sure he got there. I was looking forward to coming back home and finding a little peace and quiet. When Dr. Pursch and Dr. Griffith told me they wanted me to stay for three weeks of family treatment, I told them I couldn't. I had to get back home to take care of the children.

Dr. Pursch sat me down and talked with me a long time. He asked me how I felt, and everything just kind of gushed out of me. I remember it was a great feeling of relief to let things out.

Finally, I agreed to go back home, make arrangements to take care of the kids and return to Long Beach for three weeks. I wasn't 100 percent sure it was the right thing to do, but Dr. Pursch assured me that it was. I was ready to believe in Dr. Pursch. He was the first person in years who had asked me how I felt.

The kids were very supportive of my returning to Long Beach. Buddy even came out with me for a week and participated in the program himself. I've often wished that all four of the older children could have spent at least a week in treatment. I've tried my best to tell Kim, Jana and Marle what I learned, but there's no substitute for being in the program yourself and looking at things from your own perspective.

I've recommended a lot of treatment programs to people with alcohol or drug problems in the last few years, but I always check first to make sure they have a strong family program. Alcoholism is a family disease. Everybody in an alcoholic family needs help.

* * *

Those three weeks in Long Beach were filled with some of the best and worst times of my life. It seems like I cried three weeks straight.

During the day, I attended lectures and was in group therapy sessions with other families and with the other families and patients together. Billy and I also had individual family counseling.

At night, I would go back to the motel where I was staying and study literature 'til the wee hours, or attend Al-Anon meetings.

It was very intense. I could tell in the family sessions with Billy how far apart we were on things, but, at least, I finally knew the cause of all the craziness in our lives. It was alcoholism. I wasn't at fault; Billy wasn't at fault; but we were both crazy as the dickens because of alcoholism.

Lord, I might even have been crazier than Billy, if that was possible.

* * *

I found out through self-discovery that I had been living as an extension of Billy for more than 20 years. I had no self-worth and no identity of my own. Everything I said or thought hinged on Billy's actions.

I had no thoughts of my own. All I lived for was to care for and protect the kids and to keep Billy from saying or doing things that would embarrass Jimmy or the family.

I had lost myself somewhere along the way. The only strokes I got were for being a good wife and mother. My whole life was based around the needs of others. I didn't think enough of myself to say no to others.

It was sickening.

A compliment for me was someone saying, "Poor Sybil, she's a good woman for putting up with all of Billy's crap."

* * *

In treatment, I learned that I did have good sense and that people would care just as much for me if I said no.

I also began to learn to trust again and not be responsible for other people's feelings and actions.

I hoped and prayed Billy would quit drinking, but I was prepared to leave him if he didn't and stand on my own two feet.

Treatment was an emotional experience for me, and at times, I felt lost and frightened. But when I left, I knew that I was beginning to become a new person, and nobody—even Billy—was going to take that away from me.

* * *

When I speak to audiences, I like to tell this story to illustrate my independence.

For years, I wouldn't wear high-heel shoes when I went out with Billy because they made me a lot taller than him. Billy never asked me not to wear high heels; I just knew he was uncomfortable when I wore them.

Well, when I went home following treatment, I bought myself a pair of the highest heels you'd ever want to see and wore them the very first time Billy and I went out together.

I must have looked a foot taller than Billy to all of our friends. And, believe you me, I felt a foot taller than I ever had before.

* * *

Even with the firm foundation I had from treatment, I knew it was going to be rough for Billy and me. And, boy, was I right.

Billy came home to a mess of investigations and the Libyan situation. I backed off to protect myself and let him deal with things the best way he could. I know he felt like I wasn't supporting him, but there wasn't any other way for me to do it. If I had tried to protect him, I would have been right back where I was before treatment.

It was like we were starting our life together all over again. I also found out what a fool I had been about our finances. We were going broke, and I couldn't believe it.

I had never once questioned Billy about our finances during the time all the money was coming in. It seemed like we were overspending, but I didn't have the courage to ask about it. I thought Billy knew what our limits were.

It was my fault for not asking, but I never made that mistake again. I asked Billy about everything, and I don't think he liked that a darn bit.

I knew all along that the changes Billy was making were as hard on him, as mine were on me. But I persevered, and Billy came to respect me for that.

Finally after about three years, our new relationship matured and became stronger than it ever had before.

Since then, I never gave a second thought to Billy's ever drinking again. We had been through almost a total transformation as individuals and as a couple.

CHAPTER SEVENTEEN

You hear a lot of people in A.A. refer to their sobriety as a miracle. For a long time, I thought that was just so much talk. I didn't see anything miraculous about quitting drinking.

But, now, looking back, I can see it was a miracle that I didn't drink in the first year or two after I got out of treatment.

I got out of treatment in April 1979 and walked into one mess right after another. There was a grand jury investigation about channeling $1.7 million from a peanut warehouse account into Jimmy's campaign; the IRS was hounding me about back taxes; and I was trying to promote some sort of import-export deal with the Libyans to get out of hock.

To top it all off, Sybil and I weren't getting along too well, and with every passing day, I was getting a little deeper in debt.

It was a mess, but somehow, I managed not to drink. I had some vague realization that if I started to drink again, things were never going to get better.

Too, I didn't want to give anybody the satisfaction of saying, "See, I told you that bastard couldn't stay sober."

* * *

All that other stuff going on at the time I got out of treatment kind of fades in comparison with the Libyan deal.

What people didn't realize was that I had everything to gain and nothing to lose by continuing to work with the Libyans in 1979. I never once considered backing away from them.

Mr. Shahati, their foreign trade minister, had called me at the Long Beach treatment center to ask me how I was doing. He also expressed his regret about all the negative publicity our association had generated for me and said he hoped they could make it up to me.

I considered Shahati, Dr. el Houderi [Libya's charge d'affaires in Washington], and a lot of other Libyans as friends and business associates. I didn't see a damned thing wrong with working with them as a private citizen. I didn't have a lot of other people willing to work with me at that time.

I knew Jimmy didn't like me dealing with the Libyans, but I had no way of knowing in 1979 how big a flap it was going to cause for him a year later.

How was I to know that Ted Kennedy, Birch Bayh and some other so-called loyal Democrats were going to use the Libyan thing to try to dump Jimmy from the ticket in 1980?

I never thought anyone would try to implicate Jimmy in my Libyan dealings. Jimmy may be a lot of things, but he ain't stupid and he ain't dishonest. I thought everyone knew that.

I can't plead total ignorance, though. Jimmy had asked me point blank not to go to Libya the second time, and [Zbigniew] Brzezinski [President Carter's National Security Adviser] had called and asked me to drop a crude oil deal that I had brewing between the Libyans and Charter Oil. Brzezinski told me the deal could prove to be embarrassing to the president.

I told Brzezinski to mind his own damned business.

* * *

Someone could write a whole book about my Libyan adventures, but I don't want to get too bogged down in details. Here's kind of a quick overview of the whole thing.

- In September of 1978, I went to Libya for the first time, and four months later, a Libyan delegation visited Plains, Atlanta, New York and a lot of other places in the U.S.
- While I was in alcoholism treatment, Randy Coleman, who was acting as my representative, met with a group of Libyan officials in Rome to discuss our doing business together in some type of import-export arrangement. I was thinking at the time about an agricultural deal—farm goods, farm implements and so on. When Randy got back, he said that there was a chance for us to act as a commission agent for a U.S. oil company of our choosing to import Libyan crude oil to America. I was a little hesitant about that at first, because I didn't know a lot about the oil business. But I didn't shut the door on it. I knew we needed oil over here, and Libya had a lot of it.
- In May of 1979, Randy and I flew to Rome for a weekend to meet the Libyans again to discuss visiting Libya during the tenth anniversary of Qaddafi's government. We also talked about the crude oil deal and the possibility of me getting a $500,000 loan from the Libyan government to keep me afloat while we were getting the oil deal together.
- In September of 1979, I went to Libya for the tenth anniversary celebration. Sybil, Buddy and five of our close friends (Norman Mallard, Jimmy and Lorraine Murray and Clarence and Faye Gibbons) went with me as guests of the Libyans. Randy joined me about two weeks later after Sybil, Buddy and our friends had gone home. Randy and I stayed

another two weeks. During that time, I mentioned to the Libyan government that we had talked to Charter Oil Company about the oil deal and delivered a letter to the Libyans from Charter.

- Nothing happened for a time on either the oil deal or the loan, but in December, Randy was able to obtain a $20,000 check from the Libyans, which we considered to be an advance on the loan.
- In March 1980, my financial condition had worsened, so I sent Randy to Libya to see if the loan could be speeded up. Mr. Shahati told Randy the loan had been approved, and about a month later, we received $200,000 from the Libyan government. I was feeling pretty good about the oil deal, which I thought would take place in early summer, and thought repaying the loan would be easy. It looked like things were turning around for me.
- In April, the Libyan government sent a cable to Charter Oil confirming the oil deal, and a copy of that cable got into the hands of the White House. That's when Brzezinski called me and asked me to pull out. Afterward, the whole deal fell apart.
- Also that spring I was asked to register as a foreign agent of the Libyan government, and I refused. I finally registered in the summer, although I still thought it was just so much crap.
- Before long, the press was trying to link Jimmy with my activities, and they were labeling the whole damn thing "Billygate."
- The Senate held two hearings on the deal. The first was a hearing on whether I received special consideration from the Justice Department in not registering as an agent, and the second was an investigation into whether Jimmy or his Administration was involved with me in any way.

* * *

I can sum up the Senate hearings in one word: bullshit.

They were politically motivated. Once the election was over, the whole thing just went away like it never happened. Nobody ever charged that there was any illegal activity by me or anybody else.

I told the Senate Judiciary Subcommittee that I welcomed the hearings. I said:

"Despite all the media fuss and the convening of the subcommittee, I see no allegations that anyone committed a crime and no indication that the Justice Department treated me with any kind of special favor."

I said I was actually treated like a hot potato by the government because I was related to the president of the U.S.

The funny thing about the hearings is that they were instigated by Jimmy's own party because some senators wanted Jimmy to step aside to make way for Teddy Kennedy or somebody else to be the Democratic nominee. [Democratic Senator] Birch Bayh gave me hell throughout the hearings. The person on the committee that I liked most was a Republican—Bob Dole. Dole treated me fairly and helped cut through a lot of the nonsense.

It took me a long time to forgive Birch Bayh. Finally, I decided to hell with it. It was all just politics.

I never did forgive William Safire of the *New York Times* or [columnist] Jack Anderson. As newspapermen, they should have been more objective than the politicians. But they printed every allegation against me as truth. You'd have thought they wanted to lynch me.

Once in New York, Safire and I had a big argument. I called him a " cheap shot artist" and accused him of carrying out a vendetta against Jimmy. I think Safire thought all people from Georgia didn't have enough sense to tie their shoestrings.

* * *

The worst thing about the hearings is that they wiped me out financially.

Because I was involved in two grand jury investigations into campaign matters and an IRS investigation, I had four separate law firms representing me at one time. It cost me a small fortune.

A private citizen can't afford to testify in a Senate hearing unless he's a multi-millionaire. It's not fair. I read somewhere that 81 government staff people and five special prosecutors were involved in the investigation against me, and that the total cost of the investigation was something like $30 million. And then they just dropped it all.

The grand jury investigations were about as bad. I was tied up with an investigation into Bert Lance's affairs in the fall of '78, and I was on a 24-hour call for four months in 1979 when the [Paul] Curran grand jury was investigating allegations that Carter's Warehouse funds were used in Jimmy's campaign.

I was never involved in Bert's affairs, and to tell the truth, I wouldn't have known whether or not campaign funds had been parked overnight in one of the warehouse accounts. There was something like $34 million in campaign funds moving through different accounts. If something got mixed up, I never knew about it.

Anyway, no indictment was ever handed down. But the investigations tied me up for seven months.

* * *

CHAPTER SEVENTEEN

One time during all the hearings I characterized myself as a common citizen caught up in a lot of uncommon problems because my brother was president. That pretty well summed up my predicament.

* * *

Thirty-eight year old Randy Coleman was even more intimately involved than Billy in the various discussions with the Libyans. He met with the Libyans six or seven times on behalf of Billy and estimates that he spent a total of four or five months in Libya and several European cities.

Coleman still rues the fact that the Libyans chose to send a cable verifying the oil deal with Charter Oil of Jacksonville, Florida.

"If that damned cable hadn't been copied to Billy Carter, we would have had a deal signed, sealed and delivered," Coleman says. "As it was the IRS was alerted, and they called Charter Oil and told them to call the deal off.

"Hell, we didn't do a damned thing wrong. It was a straight business deal. Nobody was being taken advantage of. America was in an oil crunch, and we were procuring oil from Libya through a legitimate company. Other U.S. oil companies were buying Libyan oil, and nobody said a damned word about it.

"Libya was going to get some foodstuff it needed, Charter was going to make money, we were going to make money, and the American people were going to get the oil they needed.

"Those hearings were the last straw for me. They were a farce. It amazed me as an individual citizen to see how dumb U.S. Senators could be.

"I testified first at the hearings and didn't even bother using a lawyer. I just told the truth, which was pretty simple when they ask you the same question 68 times and it takes them four days to interchange information between the Justice Department and the Senate.

"The final time I testified, people stood up and clapped when I finished.

"I was proud of Billy at the hearings. He never backed down once — but then again, I never expected him to. Billy always knew how to deal with people because he always knew where he stood. He was a point-blank, straight-up guy with farmers, Senators, Libyans, everyone he dealt with."

* * *

People always thought I got rich off the Libyan deal because of the $220,000 I received from them.

That was a drop in the bucket compared to my legal and travel expenses and the loss of income I suffered. My only occupation for a steady two years was preparing for and testifying at investigations.

I always considered the $220,000 an advance on the $500,000 loan Mr. Shahati had arranged. We never signed any papers, but my understanding was that we would once the import-export deal was finished.

The Libyans never once asked me for repayment. I think they considered the money payment for all the mischief my relationship with them had caused me. I never looked at it that way. To me it was a loan, which was to be secured by a mortgage against my house, and I had every intention of repaying it when I was able.

I paid back some when I got a little bit ahead, but that was all I could manage.

* * *

One thing that really bothered me about the whole Libyan thing is that people got the impression I was anti-semitic.

A picture in *Time* magazine of my first trip showed me looking at a map with Mr. Shahati and said he was pointing out the location of Israel to me.

If he was, I don't remember it. I never looked at the trip as an Arab vs. Israeli thing. And I sure as hell never discussed C-130 transports or any government or military matters with the Libyans, or Jimmy.

The media raised the anti-semitic fuss and badgered me with it everywhere I went.

I just wanted the whole issue to go away, but then I got drunk and blurted out that there were more Arabs than Jews at that New York reception. Everybody really jumped on me then.

Well, I'm not anti-semitic. I'm not anti-anything. I've always said I ain't prejudiced about who I like and don't like. I don't care if someone's black, white, pink or green, or a Baptist or a Muslim.

* * *

Billy's close friend Charles Harris, a Georgia Democratic party leader and a member of the University of Georgia Board of Regents, is Jewish. He says:

"I didn't like Libya in 1979 and I don't like them now, but I defended Billy against charges of anti-semitism from the moment I heard he was working with the Libyan government. There's absolutely no bigotry in Billy. He has never intended any harm against anyone in either mind or body.

"If Billy had asked me, I would have advised him against going to Libya

because of the harm it could do to both him and Jimmy. But for all of Billy's omissions and commissions, I know for a fact he's not anti-semitic.

"We don't have a synagogue in the little town of Ocilla where I live, so a group of us from small towns meet on Saturday nights all over South Georgia. Once when we met in Cordele, which is about 30 miles from Plains, Billy and Sybil joined us, and they sat there for two hours and soaked up everything that took place.

"I could tell that night how much respect Billy and Sybil had for Judaism and other religions.

"After the Libyan affair, when Billy wasn't receiving any speaking engagements, I invited him over to Ocilla to be grand marshall in our annual Sweet Potato Parade. He helped bring out the biggest crowd we ever had—about 15,000 people.

"He was a very popular man in Georgia and in the South. And I loved and respected him."

* * *

I was also mad at how some of Jimmy's aides handled the Libyan situation.

Some of them wanted Jimmy to disavow me.

Jimmy's Press Secretary Jody Powell was always real loyal to me. Once Jody had to put out a press release critical of something I had said, but he called me beforehand to let me know about it. I told Jody I understood.

Jody comes from the little town of Vienna, not far from Plains. Some other people on Jimmy's staff were from around here, too. They helped get Jimmy to the White House, and I think Jimmy would have been better off if he would have continued to rely on them more in the second half of his term. Instead, he turned more and more to the Washington insiders.

I think Jody, Phil Wise and the others understood what it took for Jimmy to keep in touch with the common people.

I really hit the roof when the campaign people tried to keep Buddy from coming to the Democratic Convention. Buddy had worked his butt off for Jimmy out in California, and they didn't want him there because of my involvement with Libya.

It was one thing to kick my butt, but they had no business taking things out on my kids.

* * *

Despite all the problems I had about Libya, I always enjoyed meeting and talking with the Libyan people, particularly the average people we met when we toured all over the countryside. I was treated courteously everywhere I went.

I never met Qaddafi. At the tenth anniversary celebration, I saw him up close from the reviewing stand. He was wearing this long flowing robe and was real animated when he was talking to the crowd. The people seemed to respond to him.

I was told Qaddafi wanted to meet with me personally, and I hung around for awhile after the others had left for a chance to meet with him. The meeting never came off, so finally I told Mr. Shahati that I needed to get back home.

Sybil and Buddy enjoyed the first part of the trip, but they were ready to go home after two weeks. There was a delay when they were leaving, and Buddy got a little nervous.

He said, "Daddy, I'm ready to get out of here."

Once we sat down to this big feast, and Jimmy Murray was really enjoying himself until he found out he was eating camel heart and beef kidney.

While we were in Libya, they took great pains to show us what the government was doing for the people. They showed us their housing projects, their hospitals, their schools, their farms, everything.

I really believe the Libyans are proud of their country.

Despite being treated well, I never had the desire to go back to Libya, even though I had several invitations.

For a long time, I didn't feel like leaving Georgia. I had had enough of the spotlight to last me a lifetime.

* * *

The only other episode involving Libya came in November 1979 when Rosalynn called me in Plains and asked if I could talk to someone from Libya about helping to free our hostages in Iran.

I went to Washington the next day and cleared the plan with Brzezinski and Secretary of State Cyrus Vance before approaching the Libyans. After about a week, I succeeded in setting up a meeting between el Houderi and Brzezinski. The Libyans agreed to try to intercede, but, of course, nothing ever came of it.

I really don't think any country could have intervened with Iran in the hostage situation, but it was worth the try.

It damned sure would have silenced a lot of my critics if Libya had been successful. But my luck wasn't running that good in '79 and '80.

CHAPTER EIGHTEEN

The Libyan problem was a colossal pain, but my problems with the IRS were just as bad in their own right.

The IRS harassed me from the day Jimmy took office and didn't let up until he was out of office. And there wasn't a damned thing I could do about it, although I tried. I fought them tooth and nail for four years running.

I probably could have saved myself a lot of grief by just paying whatever they said I owed. But I told them to go to hell.

If there was any consolation for me, the IRS spent ten times more investigating me than they ever got from me.

What made me mad is that they kept searching for fraud. The state director and some of the agents thought if they could prove fraud against me, they'd get a lot of publicity and maybe a promotion. Too, I think they just enjoyed having power over somebody connected with the president.

* * *

I knew the IRS was powerful, but I had no idea how much power they had. It's frightening. They are a law unto themselves. They can do any damned thing they want to.

They can garnish your wages 100 percent, "red tag" your property, harass your family—anything. Even the lowest-level agents go around like they think they're God.

They scared our kids half to death, following them around in unmarked cars and calling and telling them they were going to sell the house and everything else we owned.

It got to the point where I had to slip out of the house and drive one of the kids' cars just to shake the agents.

One time I invited two agents, who seemed reasonably friendly, into the house for a drink, and the very next day, the two agents got transferred.

The IRS harassed my sister Ruth, too, which proved to me that the whole thing was politically motivated.

* * *

Billy's accountant Donnie Roland also believes the IRS investigation of Billy was politically motivated.

"Plenty of late income tax returns don't receive full audits or investigations," Roland says. "The IRS likes to make examples of celebrities, and Billy just walked right into trouble with them because of his sloppy personal records and poor attention to detail. Billy always said he was too busy to keep records. He would just hand me a wad of receipts from time to time.

"We never did deny that Billy owed additional taxes because of his lack of records, but the IRS refused our initial settlement offers. They kept looking for fraud, which simply wasn't there.

"We settled with the IRS in 1981 for about $200,000. Most of the money Billy paid was for penalties and interest and taxes from two corporations in which he was involved. His personal returns were pretty clean, except for a few adjustments and some untimely filing penalties.

"Even after we settled, though, they continued to harass Billy for another four years. They kept trying to prove the Libyan loan was income rather than a loan. I think we've finally laid that to rest.

"What was ironic was that Billy had negative income for two of the years they audited him. I don't know how they intended to collect fees from someone who was insolvent."

* * *

By 1981, I had no means of paying the IRS even if I had wanted to. So the IRS just swooped in and "red tagged" everything I had—the gas station, bank accounts, cars, you name it.

What made things even worse is that they were so damned arrogant about it.

My son-in-law Mark was leasing the station from me at the time, and the damned agents wouldn't even let him go inside the station.

I finally just said to hell with it; let the IRS have it all. Maybe then they'll leave me alone.

Luckily for me, Don Carter and a bunch of my friends saved me from my stupidity.

* * *

Don Carter said he couldn't believe it at first when Billy told him that he had decided to let the IRS take his property and auction it off.

"I told Billy that the IRS would sell the property for about half what it was worth to satisfy their claims," Carter says, "but he said that was fine with him. He just wanted to be done with everything.

"When I saw he was going to go through with it, I called Arthur Cheokas, Nookie Meadows and Jimmy Murray and told them we needed to put up some money to bail Billy out. Not a one of them hesitated for a moment.

"We each put up cash and paid off the IRS the next day. I took title to Billy's property, and we liquidated in an orderly fashion. We sold the properties, paid off debts, paid ourselves and gave Billy what was left over.

"When all the dust had settled, I got a note from Billy. All it said was: 'You saved my life.' I bet a lot of other people got notes, too."

* * *

Dixie Hall also came to Billy's aid.

She contacted the IRS to see if she and her friends could make a direct payment on Billy's behalf and then set out to raise $50,000. She organized a month-long yard sale at her and her husband's Fox Hollow estate near Nashville, and she and Tom T. organized three benefit concerts for Billy in Georgia.

"It was an act of friendship, pure and simple," Dixie said. "Billy was in trouble and needed to raise money. He would have done the same thing for us if we needed it.

"I never asked his permission because I knew he might turn me down.

"We did concerts in Atlanta, Gainesville and Americus. Johnny Cash, Jeannie C. Riley and others performed. They wanted to help Billy, too. All of us—the Cashes, the Carters and the Halls — were like family. If someone needed help, you just did it; no questions asked.

"We raised the $50,000 and sent it directly to the IRS."

* * *

After Don, Dixie, Tom T. and the others helped me put all of the IRS mess behind me, I decided it was time for me to find a job.

I was pretty comfortable with my sobriety then and was full of restless energy. I did some promotional stuff for Ernie Potter, a friend of Jimmy Murray's who was in the wood molding business in Americus, and then went to work for Don Tidwell in Haleyville, Alabama, in June of 1981.

I was a spokesman for Don's company and traveled all over the country promoting mobile homes, furniture and refinishing jobs for private airplanes.

The only drawback to that job was that I was on the road six or seven days most weeks. Instead of going home to Buena Vista, the company would fly Sybil and Earl out to be with me for a day or two.

The job with Tidwell led to a job with Scott Housing, a mobile home manufacturer in Waycross, Ga.

I was with Scott from September 1982 to November 1985. I was director of marketing and then vice president of marketing and was pretty well involved in all the day-to-day operations of the company.

I wanted to learn the business from top to bottom, and I became a workaholic. I would get up at 2 or 2:30 in the morning and be at work at 4 or 4:30 and work up until eight or nine at night. I was addicted to work. I guess it was some sort of substitute for drinking, although I didn't feel that way at the time. I felt like I had to make up for a lot of lost time and that I needed to get us on our feet again financially.

I think I was also motivated by guilt for all the crap I'd done.

Sybil wasn't much happier in Waycross than she had been when I was drinking, but I think she was just glad that I was sober and more attentive to the kids.

* * *

While we were in Waycross, I decided to go into a 50-50 partnership for five mobile home lots in Georgia and South Carolina.

I thought this was my chance to run my own business and really make a go of it. But it was too good to be true. My partner and I couldn't get along, and we decided to split up after only six months. I wanted to buy him out, but instead, he bought me out and then declared bankruptcy a little bit later.

After he declared bankruptcy, I was stuck with about $100,000 in debts run up by the company when we were partners.

I finally paid off all the debts, but I felt like I was back at square one.

* * *

I went to work with Ocilla Industries in June of '86. I worked for them at a plant in Waco, Texas, for a while and then became manager of their plant in Arabi, south of Plains.

It was a good move for us, and after working at Arabi a while, Roger Snow, the president of Ocilla, moved me over into the marketing department as a Public Relations Consultant.

* * *

CHAPTER EIGHTEEN

Roger Snow had first met Billy in 1982 when Billy was working for Tidwell, and they took an immediate liking to one another.

"Billy was known in the trade as an aggressive promoter," Snow recalls. "Promotions were all he was doing for Tidwell, but when he went to Scott, he went way beyond promotions and earned a reputation as someone who really 'packed his gear'—a real pro.

"When he went to work at Ocilla's Arabi plant, it was in real trouble, but he held it together. The plant managed you as much as you managed it, so it was no wonder Billy put in long hours there.

"The Arabi plant was a waste of Billy's marketing talents. I always said he did a good job in the wrong job at Arabi, but I wanted him in marketing. He and I probably disagreed on things as much as we agreed, but there wasn't a finer, brighter, more up-front person in the world to work with.

"The people who worked with Billy were very loyal to him, and he brought in business. He was great at dealer shows. I told him he was more than just another pretty face. He knew the business and had a feel for people that was rare.

"Before I met Billy, I thought he might be kind of shallow and lazy. But was I ever wrong. His depth surprised me, and he had great desire and a commitment to doing a good job.

"Some people thought I was being charitable to keep Billy on the payroll after he got sick, but that wasn't the case. He earned his keep in the Nashville and Atlanta shows alone."

* * *

By the time I started working with Ocilla, I was really used to not drinking and had started to enjoy talking about my alcoholism and working with other alcoholics.

I ain't the greatest speaker in the world, but I think the common people can relate to me.

I had made a pledge to myself when I left treatment that I wouldn't start talking publicly about my alcoholism until I had been sober four or five years. There's nothing worse than celebrities talking to people about their alcoholism or drug use and then falling on their butts again.

There are enough mixed messages out there anyway—like beer advertisements using ex-jocks.

The first time Sybil and I talked in any depth about our problems was in 1984 for Dennis Wholey's book (*The Courage to Change*). I began then to see the value in talking about my alcoholism. People would come up to me everywhere and talk to me about their problems.

I also began meeting a lot of ex-drunks. When we talk to each other, we just cut through all the preliminaries, and within an hour, we feel like we've known each other our whole lives.

Some of the best speakers I've ever heard on alcoholism aren't celebrities. They're recovering drunks from all walks of life. Only people in A.A. have ever heard of them.

Anyway, I decided to do what I could, and maybe make sort of a career out of it. I was tired of working 12 or 16 hours a day and wanted to be near my family and friends for the first time in 10 or 12 years.

* * *

Things didn't work out like I planned because of the cancer, and maybe they never will.

But I'm bound and determined to keep plugging along a day at a time for as many days as I have left.

* * *

Billy gave his last speech on alcoholism at the opening of the new CareUnit of South Florida treatment center in Tampa, Florida, on July 13, 1988. More than 400 people turned out to hear him.

In August, he did an interview in Plains with Neil Scott, editor of Alcoholism and Addiction Magazine. *Billy never saw the article. Copies of the magazine reached Plains, Georgia, on September 26, the day of Billy's funeral.*

CHAPTER NINETEEN

Sybil

October 20, 1988

Yesterday, Earl and I were sitting at the kitchen table having coffee and talking. As we sat looking out the window, three doves flew into the yard.

We looked at each other and said almost simultaneously:

"Daddy's doves are back!"

During the winter months a year earlier, Billy had fed the doves and other birds in our yard, and we would all sit around the table and watch as the squirrels and birds enjoyed the sunflower seed Billy had put out for them.

When springtime came, the doves flew away. Billy was always joking about having a dove shoot on the front lawn once hunting season started, but nobody took him seriously.

Those doves will always be "Daddy's doves" to us. Earl and I will feed them this winter in hopes that they will return again.

* * *

Billy, the children and I have discussed many subjects around the kitchen table, and now I sit with my coffee reliving those conversations, especially those of the past few months. I know I'm searching, trying to find solace for the hurt and the sense of loss I feel.

I've been thinking about how much Billy enjoyed Earl's Little League baseball games this past summer. No matter how ill he was, he never missed a game. Baseball was Billy's favorite sport, and he was happy that Earl shared his love of the game.

Billy pushed himself to do things he really didn't feel strong enough to do. He never regained his strength after the Interleukin-2 treatment at Bethesda in May.

* * *

During the summer, feeding the fish in a small pond in front of Jimmy's house became an everyday ritual for Billy and Earl.

I can see them now heading out into the summer heat and swarms of gnats—Earl in his jeans and Los Angeles Dodgers cap, and Billy with his walking cane and straw hat. The two of them literally willed those fish to grow. They fed them everything in sight.

Once, they asked me for old bread, and I gave them some left-over biscuits. As they came in the door after feeding time, they were both giggling. They told me how the fish came up out of the water begging them not to give them any more of my biscuits.

Billy said the biscuits were so hard we should be using them for doorstops. He and Earl were always teasing me about my cooking. I knew who the instigator was.

Billy and Earl began to measure the fish with home-made cane poles. They were always arguing about whose fish was the biggest. They tried to rope me into being the judge a few times, but Billy said that wasn't fair because I would always pick Earl's fish. I finally compensated by saying Earl's fish was the biggest, but Billy's was the prettiest.

By the end of the summer, Jimmy and Billy decided the fish were big enough to keep, and we caught our supper for a fish fry at Jimmy and Rosalynn's.

* * *

Billy also developed a passion for gardening. He planted tomatoes and peppers in our flower beds and kept us all busy watering and weeding. If we complained, he would smile that devilish grin of his and say we needed the exercise.

He also planted flowers for the first time in his life. Buddy gave him bulbs for his birthday, and he planted them by the driveway. Billy enjoyed watching them grow and bloom.

Billy quickly became an expert gardener, just as he did with everything he tried. And he didn't mind pointing out his talents to anyone who asked.

* * *

We had some good visits this summer with all the children. Buddy, Marlene and Will came down for vacation from Tennessee, and Marle and Jody visited from North Carolina.

I think each of us was terribly conscious of the fact that we were storing up memories, but we all tried hard to act as normally as possible.

Each day, I watched Billy literally devouring everything the children and grandchildren said and did, as though he couldn't get enough of their faces and voices. He would become visibly tired every night, but he stayed up as long as he possibly could. Finally he would go to bed, only to toss and turn and sleep very little most nights.

Many nights, we talked until dawn, always with the light on. Neither one of us liked the darkness.

It's surprising what you remember in the middle of the night. Virtually every night, we recalled some episode about one of the children.

* * *

One night we began laughing about Gloria repairing Kim's hem in church one Sunday with chewing gum after Kim caught her heel in the hem. Kim was about eight at the time and was mortified.

We recalled Buddy's first experience with cussing. Billy had bought Buddy a popgun, and Buddy had wandered off to a small pond at the foot of the hill where we lived in Macon. I began searching for Buddy and finally found him standing by the pond crying. I was frantic at first, thinking he was hurt or that a snake had bitten him. Finally, he blurted out, "I threw the damn gun in the damn pond because the damn bird I was hunting flew away." Even though I thought it was funny, I spanked Buddy for wandering off and for cussing. That night, Buddy told Billy I had spanked him for cussing, and Billy thought it was hilarious. Billy said, "Sybil, what do you expect? He learned at the knee of a master."

We talked about Jana slipping in the bathtub and breaking her front teeth and how she looked up at us with a little snaggle-tooth smile through the tears after she had fallen. Until Santa finally brought her two front teeth, she had quite of bit of trouble in school trying to pronounce certain words.

We laughed about Marle prissing off from home one day when she was about five to see her Daddy at the warehouse. I was frantic when I couldn't find her, but Marle explained to us that she wasn't alone. She said Mrs. Beasley (her doll) was with her.

Billy talked a lot about Mandy's talent as a writer and said he thought she must have inherited her good looks and talent from him. Mandy had a lively imagination as a child, always pretending and making up stories. We thought that was probably her way of contending with three older sisters and an older brother who bossed her around all the time.

We also recalled how Billy had rushed into the delivery room with his feet tangled in his hospital greens when Earl was born. Billy had been down the hall in the hospital playing poker when he learned Earl was about to make his appearance and didn't have time to change into his greens. True to form, Billy had also been making book on the sex of the baby. Billy also liked to talk about what Earl would be when he grew up. It was as though Billy were trying to form an image in his mind of a grown-up Earl. I will forever treasure those late-night talks.

* * *

As his July 5 check-up at the National Cancer Institute in Bethesda approached, Billy began to become tense and irritable. I knew he was worried.

I wanted to be with him in Bethesda because he was still weak physically, but he refused to let me accompany him. I finally convinced myself that he needed the time alone in order to prepare himself for whatever was to come.

On July 7, shortly after noon, Billy finally called to tell me the CAT Scan was the same; the tumor hadn't grown. Billy said the doctors were considering the possibility of another interleukin treatment in October after he had regained some of his strength.

The next few days were wonderful for us. Billy's spirit seemed to be renewed. He was positive and hopeful. We left Plains on July 10 by car to travel to Florida for a speech at the new CareUnit treatment center in Tampa. We took Earl with us and had a great few days at the beach in St. Petersburg.

When we returned from Florida, Billy began to become nauseated quite often, and we checked him into the hospital in Albany for more tests. Doctors discovered an ulcer and began treating that. Billy was released from the Albany hospital on July 30 and began preparing to return to Bethesda for another check-up on August 10.

As the Bethesda check-up approached, Billy became agitated and cross again, and we were all at a loss to help no matter how hard we tried. I know Billy went through a mental hell for a year, and it hurts me every time I think of it.

Again, Billy insisted on going to Bethesda alone so we made

plans for Earl and me to go to Charlotte, North Carolina, to visit Marle and Jody. Billy would join us there after his check-up.

The scan was unchanged again, but Billy developed chills and fever upon arriving in Charlotte. His temperature shot up to 104 degrees. We took him to the hospital in Charlotte, and the doctors ran some tests, which revealed nothing significant. The fever subsided after an hour or so, and Billy was anxious to check out because he had promised Earl that he would take him to a baseball card shop Earl had discovered on an earlier visit. The rest of the visit went well. Billy even felt well enough to have some friends, the Myszaks, over for a cookout before we returned to Plains on Sunday.

Still, I was concerned about the sudden fever. Things didn't seem to being going well despite the test results.

* * *

We spent the next three weeks working in the yard. Billy enjoyed watering his flowers and feeding the hummingbirds.

On the mornings Billy felt good, Leon would come by, and he and Billy would go for breakfast and a shopping trip to Wal-Mart in Americus. Billy should have done a commercial for Wal-Mart. He always said if Wal-Mart didn't have something, you didn't need it. He would stock up on birdseed, fertilizer and anything else he thought he needed. I never knew what he would bring home.

I would try to get Billy to take a nap, or at least rest, in the afternoon, but usually he would refuse. He told me he didn't want to waste his time sleeping. He was frustrated because he didn't have the strength to do the things he wanted to do.

The highlight for Billy was when he would feel good enough to go to work in Ocilla, which is about 90 miles east of Plains. Either Leon or I would drive him to Ocilla, and he would spend the day meeting and talking with his co-workers. I will never forget the love and support of the people at Ocilla Industries throughout Billy's illness.

* * *

There were calls and visits everyday from friends. I don't think Billy ever realized just how many friends he had. He had helped many people through the years in one way or another, and many of them never forgot it.

Billy received hundreds of cards and letters all during the year.

In one day while he was a patient at Emory University Hospital, Billy received cards from 38 different states. He was amazed that people he didn't even know took the time to write or send a card. I could tell he was really touched, but he tried not to show it. After all, he always fancied himself as a real hardnose.

* * *

On Sunday, September 4, Billy's fever returned.

We hadn't gone to church because Billy didn't feel up to it. I had tried to tempt Billy into eating by cooking a big breakfast, but he didn't have an appetite. I was really worried about his lack of appetite. He had eaten very little the past week. I had tried everything I knew and everything the doctors had suggested to get some nourishment into Billy, but nothing worked. He was just wasting away.

In the afternoon, our friends James and Faye Steverson from Buena Vista stopped by to visit, and when Faye hugged Billy as they were leaving, she commented on how warm Billy felt.

Sure enough, Billy had a 104° temperature. I called the doctors in Bethesda. They told me to take him to the hospital immediately, so we drove to Albany and checked him into Phoebe Putney Hospital.

We were both worried, but tried to remain calm. Dr. Phillip Roberts, our physician at Albany, ordered some tests, including a CAT Scan.

On Tuesday, the results of the CAT Scan came back. The tumor on the pancreas had grown considerably and had spread to the liver. Dr. Roberts said Billy probably had less than two months to live.

Billy and I both went into a state of shock when Dr. Roberts told us the result of the scan. I felt like someone had punched me in the stomach. I couldn't breathe and couldn't bring myself to look at Billy.

When I finally did summon the courage to look at Billy, he had this incredible look of disbelief on his face. We had grown accustomed to the scans showing no change and knew that as long as the tumor didn't grow or spread there was hope that further treatment could eventually work.

Neither Billy nor I could believe how much the tumor had grown in only three weeks' time.

* * *

CHAPTER NINETEEN

Billy immediately latched onto the hope that he could undergo a second interleukin treatment, but toward the end of the following week, Dr. Rosenberg told us he didn't think Billy could withstand the treatment.

Billy had put all of his hopes into returning for the second treatment. Now they were gone.

* * *

Billy was suffering from intense abdominal pain and had to be heavily medicated, but he remained as upbeat and self-sufficient as possible.

At night, I begged Billy to let me stay at the hospital with him, but he would always say, "I want you to go home and be with the children. They need you."

During the days, we enjoyed being together. Billy would pat the bed for me to come sit beside him, and many times, we never said a word. We just held hands and felt close to each other.

It's hard to smile when your heart is broken, but we tried to do it for each other and everyone else who came by to visit. The children came to visit when they weren't working or in school. Billy was insistent that they keep their regular schedules

Buddy came down from Tennessee to visit, and he and Billy were able to spend some time alone together. I know Billy was grateful for that.

* * *

While Billy was in the hospital, Marle had her baby—William Luke. We had planned to be in North Carolina for the birth, but, of course, we couldn't make it.

We got a call bright and early on September 8 informing us that Marle had gone into labor. We were both excited and kept the phone lines hot. My heart was full. I knew what Marle was going through, and I swear that I even felt some sympathy labor pains.

By late afternoon, everyone on our floor knew we were expecting a grandchild. Doctors, nurses and even a few patients were stopping by for news. Finally, around seven in the evening, Marle delivered a fine son.

Billy shed a few tears when he learned that his third grandson had been named for him and his paternal great grandfather.

Billy, though, managed to provide a little levity to the situation.

He reenacted his first conversation with Marle after the baby had been born. She had had a C-section and was on medication for pain, and Billy, of course, was on medication, too. He said they were both so high that neither one of them knew what they said to each other.

He said, "If we had been on the street somewhere, we would have been arrested."

* * *

We kept Marle from knowing the seriousness of her father's condition because of the imminent birth, but a few days after she delivered, Marle asked me pointblank over the phone how Billy was.

I couldn't skirt the truth any longer. I had to tell Marle that the doctors had said Billy had less than two months to live. I was trying hard to come to grips with the truth myself and still hadn't told Earl.

I never could bring myself to give Earl a time frame. I just let him know that Daddy would not be with us for very long. Earl was then, and is now, a trooper. He was constantly looking after my needs, urging me to rest and doing his best to act normal around Billy. His courage served as an example to the rest of the family.

I was proud of how all the children handled the situation.

* * *

Kim was pregnant, too, and was due on Christmas Day. Billy said he wished he could live to see the new baby. Kim's daughter, Little Mandy, drew Billy pictures of what she thought the baby would look like.

Billy said, good, now he knew exactly what the baby would look like and hung the pictures on the wall of his hospital room.

* * *

It's so hard to keep your sanity when every second is so precious. You want to make every moment special.

The tears were flowing constantly for me inside, but outwardly I was in control of myself.

I know I couldn't have lived through Billy's illness with my mind intact had it not been for my faith and the lessons I learned through family treatment at Long Beach when Billy was in treatment for alcoholism. I learned to live one day at a time and to try to be the best person I could for that day.

I also became painfully aware of how precious life is.

As sick as Billy was, he still had the strength to talk to me and help me recognize the responsibility I had to the children. I knew I had to be strong, but I don't think I will ever be as strong as Billy was throughout his whole ordeal. He had such courage.

* * *

Visits from family and friends helped the days go faster in the hospital.

Our minister, Brother Dan Ariail stopped by often and just kind of rolled with the punches when Billy tried to shock him with his language.

Tom T. came to see Billy shortly after he was admitted to the hospital and stayed for a few days.

There is nothing to compare with the love of a true friend, and Tom T. and Billy had that special relationship. They understood each other and were so much alike in many ways. They were totally at ease in the presence of each other. They might sit for an hour and not say a word, or they might tell stories for hours on end. They both had a great penchant for story-telling, and the taller the story the better.

Johnny Cash called Billy in the hospital one day, and the next day, Jesse Jackson called.

I remember Billy saying, "Damn, I can't believe they took the time to call me."

* * *

It became evident by the end of his second week in the hospital that Billy's condition was worsening.

But Billy was ready to go home, and we all wanted him at home. The doctors prescribed the continued use of antibiotics, and we made arrangements for nurses to come by the house to administer them.

Billy left the hospital on September 19. I shall never forget the ride home from Albany, which is about an hour's drive from Plains.

We were both happy to be going home, but we made the trip home in total silence.

From the look on Billy's face, I knew I shouldn't intrude on his thoughts. It seemed as though he was memorizing every inch of the countryside with which he was so familiar.

He lowered the car window and let the breeze blow across his face. I remember being concerned that he might catch cold, but I didn't say a word.

I left him with his thoughts.

* * *

When we arrived home from the hospital on September 19, everything was ready for us.

Our good friend Nookie Meadows had a hospital bed set up in our bedroom so Billy would be as comfortable as possible. We placed the bed by the window so Billy could look out on the front lawn and watch his birds and squirrels.

He could also watch our next-door neighbor, Howard, mow our grass. Everyone in a small town like Plains pitches in when someone is ill. Meals are cooked and brought to your home; errands are run; your house is cleaned. What a blessing it was for us to have such friends and neighbors. I will forever be grateful that we had moved back home to Plains before Billy became ill.

* * *

I was glad to be back in my kitchen because I wanted to prepare something Billy might enjoy. It had been weeks since he had eaten normally, and his weight was down to 125 pounds, from 184 just a year earlier. It broke my heart when he couldn't eat; he had always enjoyed good food so much.

Billy tried to sit up in his favorite chair in the den, but it exhausted him so that he agreed to stay in bed. He kept saying that he didn't want to be a burden to me. I had to leave the room every time he said it.

I used to tell Billy teasingly that he was either the cleanest or the dirtiest man on earth because he took at least two showers or baths a day—sometimes more. He loved to stand under the shower and let the water rain down on him.

I cried when he could no longer stand to take his shower. But I helped him get his two baths. I wouldn't let anyone else help him. Billy responded by telling everyone I was after his body.

He never stopped the wisecracks.

* * *

When school started, Billy had made a bet with our grandson, Little Billy. Billy said he would pay Little Billy $5.00 if he could go for two weeks without getting his name on the blackboard for talking in class.

Billy probably felt like it was a safe bet. Little Billy is a red-headed second grader with an awful lot to say.

But Little Billy fooled his Grandaddy. He managed to accomplish his goal on the Friday before Billy came home from the hospital on Monday. After school on Monday, Little Billy came over to the house and hustled in to see Billy.

Billy was tired from the trip home, and I ran everyone out of the bedroom so he could get some rest.

Little Billy kept coming back to the bedroom door to see if he could come in. After I refused him a couple of times, he finally took the bull by the horns and yelled, "Grandaddy, I didn't get my name on the board."

It took Billy a few moments to realize what Little Billy meant, but finally he smiled and said, "Sybil, get my wallet. I owe this boy $5.00."

Just like Billy, all of our children and grandchildren never forget a wager.

* * *

Nurses came by every eight hours to administer antibiotics to Billy, but his condition wasn't improving.

Dr. Roberts came up from Albany to examine Billy and run some bloodwork. After the examination, Dr. Roberts told me that he thought Billy had only a few days left.

I didn't tell Billy what Dr. Roberts said, but I think he knew.

* * *

Marle and Jody arrived on Wednesday afternoon from Charlotte with their new baby, and we were all happy that Billy was able to hold him.

Also, three of Billy's good friends—Clarence Gibbons, Nookie Meadows and Don Carter, came by to see him. Billy was able to talk with each of them for a while, and I think it really lifted his spirits. They made him feel a part of everything that was going on in their lives.

I think he got to them, though, when he asked them to be pallbearers at his funeral. He was in charge of his own arrangements almost to the very end.

* * *

When Dixie Hall arrived from Nashville, I could see the sense of relief on Billy's face because he knew Dixie would be there for me.

Of course, the children, Jimmy and Gloria were there for me, too, but Dixie and I had weathered many a storm together, and she has always been to me what Tom was to Billy—a no-questions-asked friend.

* * *

With the arrival of Buddy and his family, all of our children were home. And Billy was aware that his entire family was with him when he slipped into a state of semi-consciousness on Friday night.

We sat with him through the night and tried to draw strength from each other.

We each had our owns thoughts and memories, but we were all praying that Billy was not in pain.

* * *

Saturday night was the longest of my life.

I tried to be happy for Billy because I knew his struggle was almost over. But I was selfish, too—like most people, I guess—because I kept wondering how I could live without him. He had been my life for 33 years.

* * *

As the new day began on Sunday, September 25, Billy left us at 7:06 a.m.

The loneliness I felt at that moment will be with me forever.

I cannot describe the feeling. Perhaps, only another person who has lost a mate can understand.

For the remainder of that day and all day Monday, I was in

somewhat of a daze, although I continued to function. I managed to make all the necessary arrangements that Billy had not already made himself.

Hundreds of people came to pay their respects, and I kept thinking, "Oh, Billy, if only you could see all the people who have come."

My children kept reminding me that their daddy could indeed see all the people.

* * *

Brother Dan Ariail, our minister; Brother Will Campbell, our beloved friend; and Tom T. Hall, Billy's soul mate, all took part in the service.

There is no easy way to get through a funeral service, but the love and concern that surrounded us that day touched each of us in a special way.

Buddy had asked me earlier if he might ask Tom T. to request that all the men present remove their ties as a final tribute to Billy. I smiled, because I knew how pleased Billy would have been. He hated ties and was not wearing one that day.

* * *

The days are long now and sometimes so very empty. But I know I have to live each day one day at a time, and the healing will come.

Sometimes I think I can't stand the pain another minute, and when that happens, I think of one particular line in Tom's eulogy:

"Lord, we believe the life of Billy Carter to be so special and so precious that our wish is to keep his memory alive with the same vigor that he mustered in living that life."

I shall.